Before You're Not Little Anymore

Vinodini Parimi

This is a work of non-fiction. Names, characters, businesses, places, events and incidents are either products of the author's imagination or used in a fictitious manner. Any resemblance to actual persons, living or dead, or actual events is purely coincidental.

First Edition: July 2019

Typeset in Helvetica

ISBN: 978-93-88698-12-2

Cover Design: Aruvi Dave

STORYMIRROR
Stories that reflect you

Publisher: StoryMirror Infotech Pvt. Ltd.
145, First Floor, Powai Plaza, Hiranandani Gardens,
Powai, Mumbai - 400076, India

Web: https://storymirror.com
Facebook: https://facebook.com/storymirror
Twitter: https://twitter.com/story_mirror
Instagram: https://instagram.com/storymirror

Praise for *Before You're Not Little Anymore*

Vinodini's book is that unique gift that offers tons of wisdom wrapped in a series of insightful anecdotes. These life lessons are personal to her and her son and yet, as you read each chapter, you will see a part of your own family members there. My recommendation? Irrespective of whether you, the buyer of this wonderful book, are the parent or the child of the house, leave it in the sitting room so that the other members too pick it up and read it. You will find Vinodini's letters to her son helps open a fresh avenue of communication in your own house too on topics that matter but you all have been awkward to talk about, whether it be dealing with peer pressure, losing in love, learning to accept your flaws, choosing your goals in life or just being a good person in an unfair world.

– Dr Roshan Radhakrishnan, Author/ Anaesthesiologist

*****

Vinodini's writing is authentic, succinct and keeps the reader engaged. I'm sure her son will treasure this book, filled as it is with wisdom and love. Her advice is applicable to all young people and a great read for parents and teens.

– Corinne Rodrigues, Blogger/ Instructional Designer/ Blogging Coach

*****

A delightful, compelling collection of letters from a mother to her son. To be cherished like a delicious bowl of porridge that will soothe you, heal you and remind you of your mother's love.

– Preethi Venugopala, Amazon Bestselling Author

*****

Vinodini writes about important and sensitive issues which some parents would not be comfortable broaching with their children. She does so with courage, compassion, and empathy, sharing personal experiences to empower her teenage son to make wise choices and decisions as he leaves the roost to study abroad. Her honest and down-to-earth speaking style conveyed in her writing makes way for an open approach to healthy discussions with her son that is valuable to any parent. I think it resonates well with adolescents too as she writes from their perspective, having been there once.

– Elly Stornebrink, Public Speaking Coach

*****

I loved reading Vinodini's letters to her son and it was absolutely heart-warming to see her pouring her love woven with fond memories and sometimes sage wisdom into those letters. I know that feeling! Later, I remember she made them into a wonderful artwork for her son's birthday. Such a perfect gift! I'm really looking forward to reading the book now!

– Vidya Sury, Collecting Smiles at VidyaSury.com

*****

Vinodini's letters to her son are like walking on familiar ground. As a parent who writes letters to her daughter frequently on the blog, I could relate to the tone of warmth, care, and concern she uses. The letter on 'Setting Goals' is particularly poignant since it traces her own journey through her career and how she uses it to share wisdom with her son as he sets out on his own path. Reading the letters will make you nod and smile if you too are a parent.

– Shailaja Vishwanath, Blogger & Entrepreneur, shailajav.com

*****

For my son Viven

Contents

Introduction

My son turns 18 on the 30th of this April. While he stands on the threshold of adulthood ready to spread his wings and explore the world, all I can think of is how he will be coping with this whole new set of experiences, and life in general when he is on his own.

All these years my son had a firm finger wrapped around his little finger, guiding his steps to lead him to become the thoughtful human that he has grown up into.

Now is the time to let the finger loosen the grip so that he finds his feet, ready to walk into adulthood empowered by the values instilled in him. The thought of that brings me a great deal of pride and confidence, with the assurance that he will do well no matter where he goes.

Growing comes with its own set of exploring uncharted territories, coupled with a frenzy of emotions that come pounding on one's young impressionable mind in the most unexpected ways.

I am reminded when I myself stepped from my environs of the cocoon of my protected upbringing. I reminisced on my own experiences and life's lessons. I felt it would make sense to write the thoughts that are close to my heart, in the form of letters to my adolescent son. Each of these letters are nuggets of my experiences and learnings, along with recommendations on how to handle various emotions and situations. These letters were inspired by strong values that my parents ingrained within me.

My son and I often have healthy discussions and debates on most of these topics. Freezing them in writing gives a new perspective and clarity, and reinforces the crux of each topic.

These thoughts keep me grounded and help me tide over the toughest of situations with my head held high. I wish that that he learns and leverages from my mistakes and experiences. I hope they work for him too. Someday when he gets stuck in a certain situation, I hope he is able to refer to the appropriate letter.

My desire is that these letters also resonate and strike a chord with you, my readers. After all each of us has been through tough times, handled them to the best of our abilities, but may do better with some of the lessons and recommendations I share here.

Dear Viv,

Hi Rockstar! How are things going? I can see that you're desperately waiting for your vacation. It's not very far though. Time sure does fly by! Look at how tall you've grown in the past few months! You're shooting above my shoulders, making me feel like I've suddenly shrunk in height!

That reminds me, today I happened to open your closet to find something I was looking for. It smelt of warm nostalgia, lying under piles of neatly folded memories from your childhood that I was momentarily engulfed with. I chanced upon your favorite blue T-shirt that you had long outgrown. You know, the one with red stripes on the collar and sleeves, remember? It made me wonder how time has raced by with such alarming speed.

It seemed like only yesterday that I had put you down from my lap, so that you could toddle around safely on the soft fluffy carpet of our living room. And suddenly as though a film was running in fast-forward mode, the toddler shot up a little every day, growing out of clothes, haircuts, and habits to finally emerge as a young man with a mind of his own. It's finally time when my no-longer-little-boy needs to wear his big sturdy boots and leave the secure confines of his home to find himself.

Due to the thought of you leaving, on a sudden whim I decided that I needed to write you a letter. The thing is, no matter how much I try wording thoughts into a verbal conversation, I find it difficult. But hey, it's so challenging to sit you down and talk to you these days!

It seems like you're perpetually on wheels zooming from one place to another, busy with studies, friends, and a million other things that seem to be urgent and important all the time.

Ideally I want to put our heads together to brainstorm ideas pertaining to growing up. Now that you're at an age where you can understand a lot of things, there are so many thoughts that I wish to tell you, discuss with you, and want your opinion on. I realize that it would take me more than one letter to convey them all to you. It would take many.

There are times that you disagree with my opinions which leads us to healthy debates that I enjoy having with you. I welcome that because I love to savor your fresh young perspective like a cup of freshly brewed *adrakwali chai*. There's always room for new ideas, although a part of me yearns that we reach for a mutual consensus. After all, a parent prefers to see a bit of themselves in their child.

Sometime between growing up from a rebellious teenager into a woman (whose tinted glasses had slipped off when she was squinting through the fog that cleared with maturity), I came to understand that life is all about how one deals with emotions and circumstances. I went through a whole lot of experiences to make me see things the way they are. You will go through your own set of experiences which will shape you.

I write about a gamut of emotions and situations that I expect you will face. Life is a cycle of situations that repeat, based on our reactions to them. I hope sharing my experiences will help you create your own signature style in dealing with circumstances, with a dash of your mother's wisdom. Hope you enjoy reading them, *Beta*!

Love,
Ma

Taming Anger

Dear Viv,

Hey sweetheart! You still seem to be mad at me for not letting you go for that sleepover at Hiren's last night. But you need to understand why I stopped you. These frequent sleepovers have been leaving you sleepless, exhausted, and cranky. You need to be fresh to prepare for your board exams. It is easy to flare up when you don't get to do things your way, but well, keeping cool has its advantages which you and I wouldn't deny, right?

This morning my phone suddenly died. Just like that, without any warning. I struggled to get it back to life, but all my attempts of reviving it were met with silence from the cold device. You know how handicapped one feels these days without their smartphones. It's like someone's cut off one of your hands.

I rushed to the nearest service center to get it repaired. The technician at the counter inspected it and asked me to leave it for the day for him to repair it and collect it in the evening. He said it was a minor problem, the details of which he did elaborate, but me being technically challenged could hardly decipher what he was saying. I bet you'd have understood him better.

With a heavy heart I left my dear phone in his care. I returned to the service center in the evening at the said time, but the technician had already left for the day. On inquiring, I learned that he had not repaired my phone and there was no one else amongst their staff who could do anything about it. I felt my blood rising. The man had given me his word. How had he dared to leave me stranded like that without my lifeline? How was I supposed to function without it? I left the store in a huff without my dear phone. This little incident ruined my entire evening. I was supposed to catch up with a few friends at a new Italian café that we were to try out, but even that could not lift my spirits.

Today I want to write to you about anger. I can already imagine you chuckling at the thought of my choice of topic, knowing how you resent my short temper. We have discussed my anger time and again, but well, sometimes it takes a lifetime for a person to change the way she reacts in certain situations. This is one quality of mine that I'm not proud of. While I am still working on the same, I would like to share a chunk of my experiences with you, so that you could start young in learning to tame your anger.

At home you have enjoyed the perks of being the only child. Your room was your own private domain. You decided whether you wanted to eat a bag of chips sitting amidst a pile of junk on your bed, or took off on impulse one fine day to clean your cupboard and arrange the books to your liking. You have had your space, your own collection of games, books, music, and gadgets that you have never had to share with anyone. You have had the liberty to choose between your likes and dislikes. You smirked at boys (and more often at girls) who you felt could not match up to your interests. I remember the time you had kept a straight face at our neighbor's son when he did not seem to know what *Game of Thrones* was all about. I noticed you rolling your eyes when you mentioned it to me after he left. I wondered then about how you would deal with people who are different from you, when circumstances would leave you with no choice but to hang out with them.

As you enter this phase wherein you would be thrown in with a medley of new people, who would comprise of roommates, classmates, and new friends from varied backgrounds and cultures, sometimes you might not have the luxury to choose the kind of people you'd like to have around you. There could be situations where you might need to co-exist with someone you can barely get along with. Likewise, the other person might also have the same kind of reservations about you. I haven't yet met anyone who does not enjoy your company, but things happen. And they happen because just the way none of our fingers are alike, each of us is made differently with qualities that make us likable or the opposite. The sooner you accept this fact, the easier it will be for you to understand the finer dynamics of relationships.

Remember the time when you had moved to Mumbai with me when I was posted there on a job assignment? You made new friends in the school there. Those two friends you would hang out with were so different from your childhood friends back home. You'd often get frustrated with their bullying ways and come home in a fit of rage. You had no option but to vent your anger on me at home, since you needed those friends in your new environment and could not dare to spoil things with them.

In a situation where you are forced to deal with someone or something that you dislike, you are likely to react with anger. Thankfully it takes a lot for you to get angry—I often wish I had your calm disposition—except for the time when you had mischievously slapped your babysitter who was trying to force feed you when you were five years of age. She had stomped off in a fury with a red cheek. You missed playing with her after she quit her duties despite some of her annoying ways. I guess it was an early lesson to you on how to treat people right, no matter how impatient or angry you were. I had given you my piece of mind on how you could not hit anyone, no matter what the reason was.

The best of us succumb to rage when driven up the wall, although there are tips and tricks one can use to avoid a showdown. Let me tell you how this emotion can be both destructive and constructive in different situations. Yes, anger can also be constructive. All it requires is channeling the anger into something productive.

While we all know how destructive rage can be, it is worth keeping in mind that a moment of anger can blur our decision-making and lead us to irreversible consequences. It always helps to walk away at that moment from the person or the situation than reacting in an unfavorable way. If that is not possible, it is best to breathe deep and remain quiet at that time. Contemplate on talking to the person in a better frame of mind sometime later. However, it is important that the matter is addressed and resolved eventually. Keeping negative emotions like anger and sorrow bottled up can be detrimental to health. Ventilate and practice doing so in a healthy manner. Release your steam gently like a slow cooker, unlike your mum who keeps bursting like an agitated pressure cooker! I am slowly trying to correct that with the help of daily meditation.

More than once in my career, I have had to deal with difficult colleagues who would impact my performance at work with their temperament issues. In my early days at work, I would react to the situation with the same ferocity that the person I was dealing with displayed, or maybe two notches higher. I would have an outburst, pouring out all that was troubling me onto the person who had caused it. My voice would go several decimals higher and so would my heart rate. With time I realized that those outbursts had only worsened the situation and they had caused more harm than help for any one of us. Given the same situation now, I try my best to keep my reactions controlled and subdued. However I give it a good thought before I address the issue again, maybe after a day or two, but this time round both of us can discuss the issue objectively minus the anger.

Talking about how anger could be used constructively, have you reflected on those times when you are faced with criticism and scorn? No matter how good you are as a person or at your work, not everyone you meet will appreciate your good qualities all the time. Some people can be downright critical about everything you do for their own reasons. It can get to a point where things might not be pleasant. It is a surefire way to get you angry. But this kind of anger is healthy. It makes you reflect on your good and bad qualities and wonder where you're going wrong. Once you've confronted the person about what he must say, go back and think through it carefully, filtering out the things that you might agree to from all that they have said. You've got to be completely honest with yourself here, absolutely no cheating. If you feel there is an element of truth in the criticism, try and work on it to improve yourself. But if you have the conviction that some of the things pointed out were false and baseless, treat them as that person's ignorance, or, better yet, feel happy about those points because those are your strengths. And probably these are strengths that have brought out the insecurities of that person on the surface, which he chose to hurl at you in the guise of criticism.

There was a time when I was teased mercilessly for

posting long status messages on Facebook. Those public jibes would make me angry and upset me. I let it pass but did not quit reflecting on it. And can you guess what the result of that reflection brought in? I realized that I probably was not writing for the right audience. Perhaps my Facebook wall and friends were not the right place and people to engage my writing with. That moment of realization led me to start writing on my blog with a renewed vigor, wherein what I write is read and accepted by like-minded people. So yes, sometimes anger helps. But you've got to direct it in the right direction.

If none of the above-mentioned works, walking away or switching off from the person and the situation that triggered it works like magic. Distract yourself with a good book, your favorite music, an interesting video, or take a refreshing walk to get away from it.

I hope this helps you stay calm and collected, with better understanding and flexibility towards new people and experiences you are going to be exposed to. Accept people for who and what they are. Do not attempt to change things or people that you have no control of. All you can do is control your own reaction to things.

I've got to go and attend Aunt Mia's call now before she accuses me of ignoring her and blows her steam! She's been upset a lot these days after she had a bitter altercation with some of her friends recently. I try to talk to her and soothe her every day to make her feel better. I will end this letter with a quote that I often remind myself with when I'm angry:

'Getting angry is actually punishing yourself with the mistakes of others.'

Love,
Ma

Coping with Betrayal

Dear Viv,

I wonder what's happening to this world. It is getting increasingly difficult to come across a decent piece of news in the papers these days. After flipping through the first few pages of the newspaper this morning, I noticed how the news nowadays is all about how so-and-so had duped so-and-so. Scams, deceit, and cons of varying proportions have taken over our lives with an alarming regularity. It set me thinking on how well equipped you are to deal with this kind of toxic environment in the world outside.

After yesterday's letter on anger, today I wish to broach the topic of betrayal. You might wonder why I am writing to you about negative emotions and situations. Well, the fact of the matter is, one needs to be cautious only in situations that bring out negative consequences. Positive emotions like happiness don't need to be managed, and are much more welcome in any situation.

Betrayal sounds like a heavy word which can destroy lives, but there are minute day-to-day instances where we are exposed to betrayal, not as offensive, but nevertheless they leave us feeling cheated. For example, do you remember the day you scored lower marks in a test than one of your classmates in school? You noticed the joy on his face when he got to know about it. I recollect how betrayed you had felt by his reaction. Just the very thought that your friend was happier that you had scored lower than him, as opposed to him doing well in the test, was a big letdown.

At times life throws us graver forms of betrayal. A friend steals your brilliant idea that you had decided on for your final thesis, a cheating spouse, a work associate who borrowed money from you failing to return it, and many such instances. Now these are unfortunate events, and no matter how cautious we are, sometimes it is purely our bad luck that they happen to us. It helps in today's world to be a little guarded. Remember, betrayal often follows trust. The person who betrays you tries to win your trust first and then plays their cards. So no matter how much faith you have in someone and how close the person is to you, it helps if you do not trust people blindly. That does not indicate that you need to be paranoid. You need not suspect every action and intent of a person. You don't need to play detective either. But it also doesn't mean that you become a soft target for people to get away with cheating you.

All I ask you is not to let emotions guide you in matters of the heart, career, and money. Be practical and rational. Listen to your instincts if you sense something amiss. It will go a long way in avoiding unpleasant situations. I know this is easier said than done, but I have learned some of my tough lessons after seeing many forms of deceits. And now I know to tread safely.

Yet, despite all this, if you still stumble upon a situation where you find yourself betrayed, it is natural to experience an outburst of uncontrollable emotions like shock, anger, disgust, disappointment, and frustration. You might ask yourself, *"Why me?"* But in such situations it is recommended that you take stock of your emotions, push them aside to be dealt with later, and focus on what you can do to avoid further damage, if at all possible.

A friend of mine once lost her ATM card. She soon started getting messages on her phone to alert her on money being withdrawn from her card. She panicked initially but soon regained her composure to find a way out. She did not remember leaving her ATM card unattended, except for the time when she was in her office, where she would keep it in her handbag. The only person around was her colleague and closest friend at that point. She also wondered on how that person had chanced upon her ATM pin.

Out of sheer presence of mind, she went ahead and reported the loss to the cops. The police probes led them to investigate the ATM booth's recorded videos. There are these surveillance cameras inside the ATM centers that normally capture videos of people who enter the booth. When she was called to identify the culprit seen in the video, she was shocked to discover that it was her most trusted and close friend from work who had done the deed! Turns out she had noticed my friend punching in the pin on various occasions and had memorized it. That had helped her in withdrawing the cash from her account, using her card that she had flicked from her bag on the sly. The offender lost her job, faced public humiliation, and was also made to pay the stolen money back to my friend. Not in the wildest dreams would she have imagined that her dear friend, whom she had trusted so blindly, would have done this to her. Thankfully her timely presence of mind of going to the cops had saved her day.

After all that I have written here, let me tell you that in a world that has a large share of selfish opportunists, you'll also come across a fair number of kind souls. People who go out of their way to help people in a selfless manner. Strive to become one of those and the good that you do for others will come back to you multiplied. Give your mum the back rub she so deserves without her asking for it on some days occasionally, and who knows, you could get rewarded with a meal of your favorite pizza, probably with extra cheese! Be kind and forgiving. Having said that, I repeat, forgive but do not forget. Use the lessons that life teaches you to avoid repeating the same mistakes again.

That reminds me, I've got to go check the fashion sale at the mall this weekend. I do hope I get a good discount on my shopping. Last time I was lured by one of those discount sales, I ended up buying stuff that did not last me for long, due to the bad quality of merchandise. I went overboard and skipped checking on the fabric quality of the clothes. I'm in no mood to be conned again. One's got to be cautious everywhere. But who knows, I might be lucky enough to spot some good deals this time round. On that note, keep your eyes wide open, stay safe, and be good.

Love,
Ma

Nurturing Confidence

Dear Viv,

I hope my letters are not getting to be heavy doses of *Gyan* for you. Even if they are, you have no choice but to read them, because your mum will say what she must say (as usual)! In this letter I will address that one quality that either makes you or breaks you. Confidence.

I have seen you evolve from an awkward nerdy boy to a confident young man, who puts forth his thoughts with an air of assured knowledge, and who questions every logic instead of blindly believing them on face value. A quality that makes me proud and yet intimidates me at times, because I need to have my facts in place before I present them to you. Gone are the days I could get away with childish gibberish to pacify you to do something. While I admire the way you have molded yourself into a self-assured personality, I would also advise you to know how easy it is at times to slip into a phase of overconfidence, if you do not make a conscious attempt to balance it.

You have experienced overconfidence while writing some of your examinations in past. Do you remember the day you wrote your English exam in the 12th grade a tad overconfidently? Well there's no doubt that you always were good in that subject. Secure in that knowledge, you ended up giving less attention to your

English curriculum and had focused more on subjects that seemed tough to you. Of course that helped you score better in those difficult subjects, but when you received the marks for English they were well below your expectations. The day you are too self-assured of a certain subject is when you tend to goof up. On the other hand, an unassuming confidence comes from weighing the pros and cons of a situation practically, and will always help you analyze things clearly and perform better.

In the future you might face various situations where your confidence might not be the same, or might waver which is natural. After all we are humans, and no one can be perfect all the time. In such scenarios, my only advice to you would be to face the situation without running away from it. We tend to escape from things that make us uncomfortable or that we're not confident about. Try, try, and try again till you master it. If you master it, you will be motivated to take up other challenges. And suppose you're not able to master it, you may regret not having tried.

Beyond academics, there will also be upheavals in your personal life and relationship issues. They may pull you down and you might end up questioning yourself at times.

One of my close friends from college, Vani, once fell for a handsome guy who was our senior in college. She was on cloud nine since this seemed to be the first time that she felt strongly attracted to someone. We would see her walk with a spring in her steps, humming to herself dreamily as she went about working on her art piece. She would take extra care in dressing well even on regular days. We had never seen her this happy.

But in the days that followed, things changed. We noticed that her mood seemed to have changed. She wouldn't interact much and would stay withdrawn, lost in thoughts. Over a period of time she lost tremendous weight, and her clothes hung loosely on her frame unflatteringly. It did not help that she was living in a hostel away from her family. We were her family in this new city. It took us some amount of patient prodding to discover that the guy she had fell so head-over-heels in love with, had turned her down since he already had a girlfriend. This was something she was unaware of. She did not take this news well and went into a bout of self-doubt and depression. It took her a long time to get over that setback. She did bounce back after a few years when she met her life partner, but that particular experience had marred her confidence to a large extent.

Remember what I've told you about how I was in my school days? I wasn't really an introvert, but I wasn't the kind who would speak up in a large group. I would prefer one-on-one conversations with people I was comfortable with. If I would be asked to speak or perform in public I would chicken out. Somewhere along the way things changed as I consciously chose to break out of that pattern. I watched, observed, and learned from people of different ages and from different walks of life. My art college days facilitated that for me to a large extent. Years later I was addressing a crowd of fashion students of a degree course. I taught them the nuances of fashion even without a proper academic qualification for the same! And did I do well? Ask my students. I am still mentoring some of them after all these years.

Observe and learn from calculated risk takers. They are self-motivated people who will inspire you in many ways. Also there's no dearth of people who try to induce you with self-doubt. Steer clear of such company. Let no one tell you otherwise. These kinds of people not only pull you down, but also often try to climb up by using your fall as a stepping stone.

That reminds me of an incident that happened to me when I had started my first job. Someone close to me who claimed to know me better than myself, told me that I wouldn't last in the job for more than 10 days due to my fickle-minded nature. I lasted in that job for over three years, and continued working on different job assignments in various companies for over 13 years thereafter. The thing is, I could have gotten demotivated by that one negative comment that came to me early on in my career, but I chose to take it up as a challenge and break out of the mold that people had cast me in. People who genuinely want you to succeed will encourage you to brave the odds and attempt to boost your confidence.

However, last but not least, confidence is an inner job that grows when you nurture it with your own efforts. It comes with practice and self-motivation. If you have the drive for it, you will go out there and take the bull by its horns! And I know you have it in you my boy. Go out and claim it with all the confidence you have. The world is yours!

Love,
Ma

Dealing with Depression

Dear Viv,

I got a call from my cousin Tarika today. She updated me about how her daughter Ria was finally feeling better after combating severe depression for years. Ria had been pursuing a Bachelors course in Physiotherapy, but somewhere along the line she realized that she was not cut for the profession. On the other hand, she was passionate about playing the guitar which had always been a side interest for her. The cause for her depression was her confused state of mind about her vocation, despite finishing her graduation. Tarika told me that the only thing that cheered Ria up was playing guitar. After a healthy debate with her family and her counselor, she decided to give a career in music a shot. She applied for one of the best music colleges in London, and, to her joy, she was selected!

I'm glad Ria could accept help to sort out her dilemma and deal with the root cause of her depression. Life gives us many chances, we only need to be hopeful and be open to accepting new opportunities.

You've heard the terms 'depression' and 'anxiety' since the time you were a child. You overheard Papa talking to his patients on the phone several times advising them on their diagnosis. I wouldn't be surprised if you probably always thought of it in a clinical way. I guess by now you're aware of how common depression affects us in day-to-day life.

These days I feel very low for some reason. There's no reason that I can place a finger on, to decide why I feel so. It's just that I don't feel stimulated by what I do nowadays. My writing has been inconsistent and whenever I attempt to write something, I cannot seem to decide what I want to write about. A writer's block of sorts I guess.

It could also be that you're leaving for university overseas in some time. That leaves me with uncertainty on how I would cope with your absence. I'm so used to having you around, taking pleasure in looking after your needs, rustling up your favorite pasta, catching up on the latest movies with you, debating on various aspects of life, and generally having fun with you. I wonder how life will be after you're gone. Bleak and uncertain. But I have willed myself that whenever that happens I will try and make the most of the time to work on myself. Give priority to do the things that I always desired to do, but never found the time.

Depression can hit you anytime, even as frequently as the common cold. I feel it is important to recognize, and working on it in a healthy manner can ease you out of it in no time.

Although not always interlinked, lack of confidence and depression sometimes go hand-in-hand. As of late, we have started to judge ourselves too harshly. Sometimes I wonder why we are so hard on ourselves. A little stumble here and there and we let ourselves roll down in the doldrums.

Look at the kind of stress kids from your generation experience. I agree that a little amount of stress keeps you on your toes, but it gets alarming when it gets deeper and starts affecting your overall demeanor. What hits me most are the reasons that trigger depression in young people these days. Peer pressure, competition, attraction to the opposite gender, low performance in studies, and work-related problems are some of the major issues that plague them. The best of us go through one of these problems sometime or other in our life. How we deal with these issues is what is important.

Excelling in studies, getting admission to the right university, and carving a successful career is just one part of life. Important, yes, for earning your future bread and butter, but scoring high grades is not the only way to do it.

It breaks my heart to see young students rashly taking their lives, just because they failed on a certain exam. There are so many ways to address an issue. If only they would have come out in the open and discussed it with someone who could guide them better. Succumbing to suicide over a few marks is a downright waste of precious life. If there ever comes a time when you feel that you've not lived up to your own expectations, call me immediately. I will help you see the many wonderful qualities that you possess, and for which you are genuinely appreciated by people around you.

When I listen amusingly to dating stories of the current lot of youngsters, I'm astounded as to how having a girlfriend or boyfriend amounts to being cool. Not having one is equivalent to something being wrong with you. I mean whoever it is who decides that cool quotient is not on the right track.

I remember a couple of years back when you were still a child, you once came to me and told me how a certain someone was 'seeing' someone from your class. Out of curiosity, I asked where they "saw each other." Did they really go out to cafes, movies, or parks to see each other like one would on a date? And you had replied, *"In the school. During recess."* I had smiled at the innocence of it all. It is a blessing to be in that phase to just see things as they are, and not delve deeper in the dynamics of relationships. Once you grow up you will discover yourself. "Seeing each other" will take a different connotation altogether.

However let me share with you a gem of advice. Despite how good it feels to have a friend/girlfriend, there is life beyond that person. I mentioned in my previous letter about what it had done to Vani when she had all her hopes pinned to one person. For your own good, let your world not revolve just around that one person no matter how special they are. There are so many interesting people, places, and experiences to explore besides them. If someone ever lets you down, remember that life doesn't stop. Dive into some activity that stimulates you mentally until you're sorted out. These are passing phases. Probably in a few years from now, you will be sharing your experience with your kids and laughing about it.

There are times I see you getting desolate in certain situations. Sometimes even seemingly insignificant issues snowball into a bigger one. So my protective maternal instincts urge me to bring it up with you and make you aware of it. All said and done, God forbid, if there ever comes a time when you feel depressed, here are a number of ways that can help you come out of it.

1. Avoid interacting or exposing yourself with the person or situation that is the root cause for your depression. If that seems difficult, do your best to distance yourself mentally from that situation. It takes a bit of practice, but is not impossible.
2. Talk about the issue with someone close. If you can't think of anyone better, I'm just a phone call

away. I promise I won't judge you for it.

3. Write about it. Read it a day after and try to understand your mind better. The easiest way to do it is to save it as a note on your phone. If you're not up to writing about it, write anything that comes to your mind. It could be a free write. Who knows? You might surprise yourself with what you come up with.
4. Listen to the peppiest numbers on your music list. If possible, turn up the volume and dance like no one's watching. Oh yes, it works!
5. Go out and get some sunshine. Soaking in some vitamin D is vital. Dark dingy places are gloomy. Now you know why I insist on drawing open the curtains to the windows in your room, first thing in the morning. The early rays of sunshine are magical for our well-being in a lot many ways. Better still, go out for a walk or a jog. Let the endorphins do their magic!
6. Indulge yourself with good food. Try out the new restaurant down the street, or, better still, whip up a creamy pasta and call your best pal to share it with.
7. Give yourself a makeover. Go for that bold new haircut that you have been considering or buy some new clothes to jazz up your wardrobe.
8. Take a weekend trip with happy people. By happy people, I mean those who make you laugh and look at the brighter things in life.
9. Binge watch *Friends* or any other TV show that cracks you up.
10. Write down a list of affirmations. Go through them every single day and genuinely believe that the things that you wish for are already yours.

As I come to the end of this letter, there is one more thing I wish to stress. No matter how depressed or stressed you are, never ever turn to any kind of habit to get momentary relief. I have 100% faith in you when it comes to this, knowing your aversion for all things addictive. But when you're in a new place exposed to a new culture and new people, the temptations may be huge. Use your fair judgment to stay away from things that could turn into long-term weaknesses. Instead, look for getting that high by doing something good for someone.

I once read about a girl who would write inspirational quotes on bits of papers and leave a few of these notes randomly in public places for strangers to pick up and read. Isn't that a swell idea to make someone's day? There are thousands of other meaningful ways that you can derive joy from, by spreading it generously. In the meantime make people around you smile, and keep smiling always.

"Noble Deeds and hot baths are the best cures for depression."

– Dodie Smith, I Capture the Castle

Love,
Ma

Handling Emotions when You're Away from Home

Dear Viv,

The weather has been acting weird for some time. Just when I feel that there is a pleasant nip in the air, and start wondering if I need to get our sweaters down from the loft, is when I realize that I have been sweating even as I write this. The climate in India has become so unpredictable, really! Almost like our emotions, isn't it? Have you ever noticed how we are governed by this one central machinery that is a part of our bodily systems? Isn't it such a complex mechanism that God has created within us? A system which guides our every action, big and small. The days you are happy you give your best to everyone, and the days you are unhappy, you just can't seem to get anything done right.

While you are old enough to handle basic emotions like happiness and sorrow, when you step out of the cozy confines of your home and land up at a new place, you might be engulfed with emotions that you rarely felt or are new to you. You might initially feel overwhelmed by the new surroundings, and the urgency of absorbing everything at once. Go slow. You will eventually fall in step with your new environment and get adjusted to it. To make the process smoother, you need to give it time. One needs the patience to absorb the newness of a place, so don't be disappointed if you feel out of place in the first few days, weeks, or even months.

I once had an intern who was training under me in one of my job assignments. She had left her hometown to take up this internship. She was a cheerful bundle of enthusiasm when she joined us. In her eagerness to do everything perfectly, she started making small mistakes in her work. This later added up to bigger blunders that could not be overlooked. On top of it, she even settled for the wrong accommodation in a rash moment of indecisiveness. The locality she lived in was not safe for women which she was unaware of, and her landlord also turned out to be a sleazy character.

She suffered burnout soon thereafter and came to me in a frazzled state of mind. Thankfully all was not lost. I sat her down and asked her to slow down, make a list of the tasks that were most important to her, and tackle each of them one at a time. The first thing she did was find a safe place to live with the assistance of some helpful colleagues. Slowly she started focusing on her individual tasks in a sharper manner. Within the next few months everything was flowing smoothly for her, and she was back to her usual self.

So I suggest you give attention to one thing at a time. This will help you focus better and pick up things faster. In case that seems to be difficult, keep a pocket diary handy in which you could jot down notes that you might need to refer to later. This is a useful habit. We sometimes think we will be able to remember things without noting them down, but that's an unreliable method of remembering information.

No matter how hard you try, things will take their own course in time. Show healthy curiosity of your surroundings. Go out of your way to meet people around you. Introduce yourself and start a casual conversation. Keep yourself approachable by maintaining an open and pleasant demeanor. In time you will find yourself settling in.

My personal observation is that most of the time we

judge people by their appearances, and we tend to be guarded around those who seem unapproachable to us. You never know why that person appears so. It could be that he or she is an introvert, shy, or simply awkward at making the first move. Give them a fair chance and get to know them better. Who knows? You could hit it off with that person once they open up to you. Remind yourself time and again that forging bonds requires a fair amount of time and effort. Do not expect it to happen overnight.

Mixed with the feeling of being overwhelmed will be some amount of homesickness. The thought of not sleeping in the same bed that you slept in for years, or eating the same food that your palate was used to, can have homesickness flooding in. Expect this from the start and brace yourself to overcome it in different ways. Skype and WhatsApp could be your best friends in this case. Call home whenever you get the urge to talk to us. Keep connecting with your long-distance friends who have joined other universities across the globe, to know how they are coping with homesickness. It might be challenging to keep pace with your friends if they are living in different time zones, although some planning can make it possible for you to be in touch with them.

Back in the days when I had moved to a new city away from home, I did not have the luxury of remaining connected with people as easily as it is nowadays through Apps like WhatsApp and Skype. We used to rely on phone calls and text messages which were quite expensive at the time.

Also it would be natural for you to compare your surroundings with those of your childhood friends, who are scattered in different universities around the world. Resist the urge to compare since each place is different. The people placed there have different dynamics individual to their location.

Visit people close to your family who live nearby over the weekend if that is possible. Hopefully in no time, you will be able to make deep connections with your roommates and classmates that can possibly last a lifetime. Some of these connections may turn out to be closer than your associations with family!

Once you've become accustomed to your new environment and as familiarity sets in, you are likely to feel the rush of freedom. The freedom to do things based on your own judgment, at your own pace, and without any boundaries is quite liberating. Soak it up. Savor it. Sleep when you feel like it. Eat what you wish to. Revel in the fact that your mum is not around to nag you to trim your nails or insist that you finish your bowl of *Dal.* You probably won't believe me if I tell you, that in no time you will miss your mum's simple *Dal* too!

Enjoy your newfound freedom to the hilt for the first few days. And then once you've settled in, be reminded that the discipline that your family has instilled in you works best, no matter where you are. They are tried and true methods of maintaining self-discipline, whether it is eating healthy, sleeping on time, or keeping yourself groomed. Once you've figured out your routine, plan a schedule and stick to it. Know that in a new place you've got to be responsible enough to take care of your own health. I do not need to tell you not to misuse your freedom. I know that you're smart enough to chalk out your own boundaries.

As you settle in, sometimes you might feel lonely despite having people around you. This can happen to the best of us in a new city. It can take just one of your favorite songs that you happen to hear or a photograph you suddenly lay your eyes on, in the passing that makes you nostalgic and homesick.

I remember I'd go out on certain weekends to the malls to kill time in Mumbai during my job assignment there. I would end up feeling miserable, seeing families enjoying their time together. It reminded me of our family outings on the weekends. I once even went to watch a movie alone at a movie theatre since I so badly wanted to watch the movie, and I had no one to accompany me. People stared at me suspiciously when I entered the movie hall and took a seat by myself. Once I got rid of being conscious of what people seated around me would be thinking about me, I sat back comfortably and enjoyed the movie. It turned out to be quite a liberating experience!

Rest assured that you will learn to cope with this feeling of loneliness in a better way as the intensity simmers down over a period of time. You might probably not get too much time to dwell on it in the middle of your studies and other activities. If at all you need to divert your attention, try to look upon something interesting to do. A new place offers lots of local avenues and flavors to explore. See if you can learn a new skill in your free time. And again, your family is just a phone call away to banish that loneliness.

You must have noticed by now that most of the emotions I have stated above are what I myself have gone through when I found myself in a new city with job assignments that kept me away from home. In my case though, I wasn't too far from home. I assume your experiences might be far richer than mine, since the varied cultures you will be exposed to will likely be quite new to you. How about recording your experiences in a journal regularly, and sharing them with us when you're home for your holidays? I would love to know the details of your new journey.

Love,
Ma

Facts about Friendship

Dear Viv,

The other day I was going through our old family photo albums. These pictures are especially precious to me now, since we no longer keep hard copies of our memories. Today most of them disappear in the backup folders of our mobile phones or Cloud.

As I flipped through the album, I noticed so many familiar faces of people who were once my close friends smiling back from the yellowing pictures. It was amusing to see how some of us had evolved from being fashion slaves to self-assured personalities. One of the pictures was of me and my friends Vani and Nimi wearing bell-bottoms. Me in polka dots, and them in stripes and checks. You must have seen those pants in retro films, the kind that hug your ass and thighs and flare as they reach your calves and ankles. I would rather die than be seen wearing something as hideous as those today!

Coming back to the subject, I realized how many of my pals I had been out of touch with. In school or college we would have sworn solemnly that only death would do us apart, and carried unreasonable expectations of growing old together, not really an unrealistic expectation since there are still some friends who stay with you for life, despite distances and different life circumstances. As the years passed by, each of us grew further apart whether due to distances or the vagaries of lives.

When you're younger, you assume that nothing would change between you and your bosom buddies. As you grow older, you realize that your expectations of your friends change. The equation you had with them when you were a kid was simpler. The only objective of friendship then was being with each other and having fun. You loved all the silly teasing, exploring new toys, and playing stupid pranks on each other. Your life revolved around planning how to sneak and hit the water-filled balloon on your unsuspecting friend!

Somewhere along the way as you enter your adolescence, this friendship goes beyond having fun. Adolescence is all about who's better than whom. You'd love to be seen with the latest smartphone before the rest of the squad. Suddenly your hairdresser has changed as the neighborhood hair saloon *chacha* who gave you your *tapeli* (bowl-shaped) haircut since childhood is no longer able to understand or give you that cool Mohawk that you now sport. Somehow your need to be ahead in the game decides the dynamics of your friendship. This is when competition, peer pressure, and insecurities start showing signs. No matter how much you want to ignore these deterrents, they will raise their head sometime or other.

While in school these issues were still manageable, but once you become an adult, you need to face these differences with your friends. Interestingly enough, these are the things that help you grow. They teach you how to remain grounded despite the competition, not be illogical while bowing down to peer pressure, and face your insecurities head on. And when you've tackled all this together with your friends, they understand you much better and love you for who you are. Such is the bond between childhood friends who have seen you grow and have grown with you.

In my first job in a fashion institute, I started working as a faculty member for computer-aided design. One of my colleagues, who is also a close friend, used to teach design concepts to the students in the institute. Her job was more stimulating and challenging than mine. It required the person in her position to possess a creative bend of mind along with the right qualifications. My Fine Arts degree made me qualified to teach design concepts. She eventually quit her job for personal reasons. The management had plans to replace her with me; however the idea did not appeal to her for some strange reason. She tried to refer some other candidates for her former position, but finally I was selected in her place. The fact that my friend had such reservations about me deserving a competent role was rather upsetting. One would expect your friend to stand up for you and want to see you grow. In this case I realized that my friend was not ready to see me in her shoes, even though she was planning to quit the job. That incident was a lesson for me. People may change in reaction to circumstances in their lives.

We parted ways with mixed feelings and did not remain in touch for a long time. Years later when I moved to Mumbai, we bumped into each other at a mall. She had moved with her parents who had settled there. There was an instant sparkle in our eyes when we recognized each other, but once again the not-so-pleasant memories of our last interaction stopped us from communicating with each other with the usual warmth.

A few years later we reconnected over social media. She was designing a logo for her work and asked for my opinion. We managed to break the ice. I received a call from her a few months later. She was wanting to move out of her parents' house and be on her own, as she wanted to be independent. One thing led to another and surprisingly we ended up being flatmates for the next several months. And today our friendship is much stronger and deeper than before. We had evolved in our perception and maturity. Such are the ways of life. Be prepared for surprises!

From here on, the friends that you make will be different. The people you attract as friends will be the ones who find this evolved you matching their wavelengths. If you observe the friends you've made from kindergarten to high school, there will be a vast difference in the type of people you drifted towards. The ones you make in the university will again be quite different. This is a healthy sign because it signifies that you are growing and evolving. This difference in the friends we graduate to subconsciously helps us grow as a person, since we learn from each person, both good and bad. That's exactly the reason why you should choose your friends wisely. You will be known for the company you keep. The quality of your friends will determine how your personality evolves while in their company.

Let me elaborate on what I mean by good company and bad company. No person is good or bad. I am not perfect, neither are you, but it is one's habits or qualities that are either good or bad. While I would not encourage you to be in the company of people with unfavorable habits, you may end up with them due to circumstances or because you appreciate one or more of their positive qualities.

You need to be very clear on how much you would allow that person to influence you. There could be a lot of good things to know about them other than their habits. Steer clear of peer pressure and any kind of emotional blackmail that forces you to try or adapt their bad habits. You've seen various friends I've had all these years. They are as different as chalk and cheese. Some are simple and straight, some are intellectual, and some are downright wild and eccentric. They vary in age and culture. I remain clear on how I make the most out of their company, while keeping my boundaries firmly in place.

My friend Ina has been a regular visitor to our house ever since you were a small boy. You have seen her smoke cigarettes in your presence. Despite being close friends, I have never felt the necessity to grab a puff of smoke from her. She has made her choices in all awareness. I have lived up to my convictions and never felt the need to share a smoke with her, even in a moment of spontaneity, just because we are close friends. She chides me every time I refuse the smoke that she offers me. She says, *"You don't seem the kind who wouldn't smoke or sport a tattoo!"* And I laugh it off. You know how I am. These are just not my kind of things. There are other things that bind me and her together and that is what matters.

A few days ago you had mentioned that one of your childhood friends had changed over the years, to the extent that you guys did not have anything in common to talk about or do together. Yes, things happen. People change and not all of them will share the same interests or sensibilities as you.

There's one principle that I stick to. I need to have people whom I can learn from and who can mentally stimulate me. And somehow most of my friends, no matter their backgrounds or thought processes, have been instrumental in becoming who I am today. I learn a bit from each of them. Things I want to be and things I don't want to be.

If you recall during your childhood days, I would warn you about a certain kid that I felt was not the right company for you, and you would insist on knowing what was wrong with them. Well, I can now tell you without any hesitation as to why I felt he was not right for you. As you mature certain things become instinctive. Your instincts guide you when you sense something wrong in the vibe of the opposite person, even if it is a child. While I used my gut feelings to protect you from wrong company, it is time you start listening to your own inner voice. Sometimes when we first meet a new person we either like them or we don't. This like and dislike is a play of your instincts. Pay close attention to it. We tend to ignore our intuition, only to regret it later when we're reminded of how the person made us feel in the first place.

I see youngsters hanging out with a wide range of friends these days. There's no harm in that unless you start slotting them as clubbing friends, just because you hang out with them only to be seen at the right places that are happening, business friends because they help each other's business flourish through recommendations, online friends who only exist in your virtual world so that they add on to the number of likes on your updates (yes this happens!) and so forth. Once you start putting your friends into slots according to your need that they fulfill, there's only so much to that friendship—that need. A friendship should be beyond that. It has to be without reasons.

You've been lucky to be blessed with some close childhood friends who have been with you throughout your rollercoaster ride of childhood and adolescence. Cherish them. Let me remind you though as I always do, people change with their set of priorities and circumstances. Let them go without trying to get possessive of them or upset about the situation. You yourself are susceptible to such changes in future as well. The nature of friendship changes, and if you're lucky you'll remain in touch, but things probably won't be the same. However, there are some you may lose touch with for years, but whenever they reconnect with you, nothing has changed. That's the beauty of some friendships!

Now is the time to be choosy about who you want to be around. One golden rule in choosing and maintaining friends should be that your friend should make you feel good about yourself. In times of self-doubt, they should boost your morale, and on occasions where you slip up, they should be honest enough to correct you.

Friendships needs to be selfless and for no reason. They should be comfortable like a pair of old socks that hug you cozily when you're cold, protect your feet from the ravages that the streets may cause, and make you feel good in them even if they have a hole or two. That kind of comfort will strike you in your first few meetings itself. Build on it and take it forward from there. And yes, don't forget that you need to be your friend's old pair of socks too as friendship is a two-way street. It will only go far if you walk in tandem with each other. Such walks end up making the journey of life sweet, enriched with warm memories and bonds to cherish for life!

I'll end this letter with this poem by Henry Van Dyke that I thought to be apt for you at this juncture.

Life

Let me but live my life from year to year,
With forward face and unreluctant soul;
Not hurrying to, nor turning from the goal;
Not mourning for the things that disappear
In the dim past, nor holding back in fear
From what the future veils; but with a whole

And happy heart, that pays its toll
To Youth and Age, and travels on with cheer.

So let the way wind up the hill or down,
O'er rough or smooth, the journey will be joy:
Still seeking what I sought when but a boy,
New friendship, high adventure, and a crown,
My heart will keep the courage of the quest,
And hope the road's last turn will be the best.

Love,
Ma

Setting Goals

Dear Viv,

During my early school days, we would often be given a school assignment to write an essay on what we would like to do in the future. I remember writing that I would like to become an astronaut when I grew up. The idea of floating in the galaxy, and watching glitzy planets and strange alien beings was probably the reason why. As I grew older, I got an idea on what kind of study and grit went into becoming an astronaut, and I soon brushed it off as one of my silly fancies!

I know the kind of dilemma you had faced within the last few years, in making up your mind about what you wanted to do in the future. We both discussed, debated, and weighed the pros and cons of different options. At your age it is common that you are unsure of your decisions and commitments, especially if it has to do with something that would be a permanent part of your future, like your vocation.

You've swung between dreams of becoming a physicist (from the after-effects of watching too much of *The Big Bang Theory*), to becoming a game designer, and then to finally discovering that you wanted to do something unconventional.

I imagined every fantasy of yours while you spoke about each with equal passion. All I want is that you be your own best version of yourself, no matter what you do. It's okay to dream. It's okay to venture into uncharted waters and dip your toes in, to decide for yourself if you are cut out for it. It is easy to get lost in a maze of daydreams, unless there is a plan in place to fulfill those dreams. You know how important that is with the rush of applications, essays, and tests for the prospective universities recently. All you have on your mind right now is one goal—to get into the best university of your choice.

Having sight of your goals not only streamlines your intentions, but also helps in working towards them step by step. Right now you are working on a short-term goal of bagging a seat in a university of your choice, though soon you will need to set your goals for long-term plans also. These goals can be both personal and professional in nature.

In job interviews, it is common for prospective employers to ask the candidate where they see themselves in five years' time. This question is aimed to find out how clear the candidate is with what he wants to achieve. A five-year plan is ideal to start with, since most of us have a fair idea on how life might be for the next five years. Charting a plan for beyond then will help in leading a more focused life. It is natural that plans can change midway, after all life is unpredictable, and we also undergo a lot of change with time. Despite that, that should not deter us from planning ahead of time.

My own career path took many twists and turns. Life is like that. After chucking my unreasonably childish desire to become an astronaut, only because I wanted to float in space wearing a spacesuit, I dreamt of becoming a fashion designer. It seemed so difficult when my parents did not want to send me away from home to study a specialized course in fashion design.

I half-heartedly gave in to their wishes and enrolled for what my small city had to offer me.

Although I graduated from one of the finest universities for studying the Fine Arts due to my flair for sketching, I finished my course but never pursued art for a long time. Somewhere in the back of my mind I still wanted to become a fashion designer. The idea of draping colorful prints and baubles on people and magically transform them into beautiful pieces of art, was what I wished to do with all my heart.

Within a few years I pursued a part-time one-year diploma course in fashion design after I got married. Studying after marriage is fairly uncommon in India but I was fortunate enough to get the chance. For some time after that, I custom-designed apparels as a freelancer. And when you arrived, I gave up on that venture to look after you.

I took up a course in multimedia to brush up on my software designing skills. Within a year I was at my first job teaching computer-aided design at a fashion institute. A year-and-a-half later, I also started teaching fashion illustration and design concepts to the same students.

I must tell you about this little incident that occurred to me that I recollect vividly. The fashion institute that I worked at had a red sofa in the reception area. Most of the staff members used to lounge on the sofa after lunch. On one lazy noon, I offhandedly commented to a senior colleague sitting next to me. I told her, "*Well looks like this is it. I'm going to retire from this place.*" What she told me remained with me till this day. She said, "*Never assume that life will always be the same. There will be a lot of twists and turns to force you out of your current comfort zone. Don't put a full stop to your dreams, because you never know what life has in store for you.*"

I wondered why she said that to me, but she was so right. Destiny had different plans for me. Within a few months, I was hired by a well-known luxury retail brand as an Area Visual Merchandiser. I managed their team of visual merchandisers for their stores in Mumbai. Since visual merchandising is about making retail spaces aesthetically appealing and commercially beneficial through proper merchandise display, most visual merchandisers need to come from a fashion background to cater to the skills required for this role. I ended up heading a team of fashion professionals who graduated from the college that I had initially wished to join, but couldn't.

And there was no looking back. It's been more than 10 years since and now I am a Head of Visual Merchandising for a well-known clothing brand. I handle the entire gamut from how a brand looks and attracts customers. It feels fulfilling to know that my life has come full circle, from the time I aspired to join the fashion industry to the time I head a team of graduates from the same college that I could never go to.

While I had never jotted down my goals, I feel I had somewhere subconsciously decided on achieving those goals. No matter how I now wish at times that had I jotted down my goals and charted a clear plan of actions to back them up at the start, it would probably have saved me a lot of detours in my career.

I hope you do not take the tumultuous route that I took. Make your list of goals right away. Include your bucket list as a part of it, whether you are taking a workshop in cinematography or taking a road trip with your friends. Note them all down. Once you're done that, tick the ones that you would like to achieve in the next year. Put a tentative date on the ones you feel might take more time to achieve. Highlight two major goals that need your complete focus even if they are longer term goals.

Tape this list on the mirror in your room or any place which catches your eye often. If you remember in my letter to you on depression, I had mentioned about creating a list of affirmations. Put these two goals on your list of affirmations and believe them to be already true. Before you know it, you will already have started working towards those goals. It makes sense to review your goals every few months and make changes, if required, in accordance with your current circumstances. Every five years, try and update your goals according to your life's phases, and work towards them slowly yet steadily.

By the way, have I told you about that one crazy goal I had in mind since the time you were a baby? I wish to set off on a world tour the day you get married, just so that I can escape the whole hype of the mother-in-law/daughter-in-law dynamics! I am just too paranoid about the type of mother-in-law I will make! Hopefully not the stereotypical scheming torturous types that you come across in the traditional *saas-bahu* serials on Indian television! Jokes apart, traveling the world is still very much a part of my agenda. I've managed to tick off a few places from my list, but that is just a tiny fraction of the world. I don't know when, but someday I'm sure to tick a lot of those places off my list. And when I'm back from traipsing around the globe, I hope that everything on the list on your mirror gets ticked off too, giving way for a fresh new list. Amen to that!

Love,
Ma

Happiness and You

Dear Viv,

Do you remember the time when you were your happiest self? Was it the day you got the news of getting accepted at one of the universities of your choice? Or was it the time you went out partying with your friends last week? And when would be the time that you think you would be the happiest? Will it be the last day of your board exams? Or will it be when you finally start your new life at university?

If I ask you the same questions a few months later, the answers will probably change. You might shrug your shoulders and give me another vague answer. Maybe a six-pack ab, right? We often see happiness as something dipped in either the wonderful nostalgic moments of the past or the exotic fabric of dreams we weave for our future.

I reckon most people out there will answer the question about when was the last time they were the happiest with, *"I'm happy today."* That's because we treat happiness as something elusive which flits by, even before we savor it full. Or happiness is something that waits for us at the end of the dark tunnel of unhappiness, that we imagine ourselves to be currently in.

What we fail to recognize is that we let yesterday pass by without realizing that it was the happiest day of our lives, and we wait for tomorrow to end, to then realize that actually that was even a better and happier day for us. The yesterday that we let go was once a today that we missed savoring to the fullest. The tomorrow that comes will also become a today and a yesterday. No matter how beautiful tomorrow seems, today is what we have now. So, wouldn't it make more sense that we treasure our today, and make the most of it before it is gone as yesterday.

I lost a dear friend from work recently after she was diagnosed with cancer. She was a young happy-go-lucky girl who was passionate about everything she did. Never in our wildest imagination would I have thought that she would leave the world so early in life.

After her death, her husband found a rather endearing way of reliving a collection of happy memories that he had shared with her in past. Despite her ongoing treatment, her husband ensured that both of them visited all the faraway places that she ever wished to go and ticked off doing all the things she ever wanted to do.

Every day he would post a picture of her on his social media account, enjoying her adventurous trip to an unexplored exotic location or even post something as mundane as savoring her favorite potato dishes. Some of these pictures saw her with a broad smile, despite her bald head after she had gone through chemotherapy. As we got glimpses of pages from her daily life, I discovered how much there was to be happy about in our daily lives. Most of us always seem to brush off these little instances of happiness as routine.

It's only after the journey of life nears the end, that we realize the preciousness of people who are our source of happiness.

We are right here in the middle of potentially happy moments. However we do not recognize or acknowledge this moment of happiness, because we're expecting something grandiose to make us happier. Greedy lot aren't we?

After the death of my friend, no matter how easy it is to forget, I keep reminding myself of the temporary nature of life as often as I can. It keeps me going as it makes me strive to make today my happiest day. I have learned to derive happiness from the little things in life. These things seem inconsequential, but they help us to become a happier person.

Happiness can be achieved from the simplest of pleasures. It can be the simple pleasure of picking up a fragrant flower fallen from the tree outside our apartment or capturing a rare picture of that parrot pirouetting on the birdbath on our terrace on my phone. I do little things that make me happy. It took me awhile to get the hang of this, after I understood that all the things that I complained about in past had made me an unhappy person. It was really the small things that I enjoyed and that I remembered fondly later.

Once you get into the practice of appreciation, you find internal happiness. This kind of joy does not depend on any person or situation to make you happy. All it needs is to open your senses and align it with how you glean happiness from it. To each his own. While I find my share of bliss in nature, knowing what you like is key. For example, music is one of the things that gives you immense pleasure. Revel in that joy. Find music in the mundane. Sing to yourself and feel grateful that life blesses you with that happiness that music offers you.

One misconception about happiness is when we believe that if we make people happy, we will be happy. Yes, giving happiness adds onto your happiness for sure, but only if you yourself are in a happy space when you're offering to make someone happy. When you are truly happy with yourself is when you can sincerely offer happiness to people and derive pleasure from that.

Let me share an amusing story about how I got thinking about this. A few years ago I googled the meaning of my first name. It turned out to be *"the one who gives happiness."* "*Vinod*" means happiness and the one who gives happiness is "*Vinodini.*" Really?! I chuckled to myself. Far from being a cause for generating happiness, I was known to intimidate people with my short temper. *"Wait a minute! Was I judging myself too harshly?"* Except for a few random events, I was generally an easygoing person.

That set me wondering whether I was really living up to my name. I consciously made an effort to make people happy, keeping my own needs aside, and catering to theirs. I started going out less with my friends, with the hope that my family would appreciate the extra time I was spending with them. Of course I loved my time with you and the rest of the family, but I was missing the fun of being with my girlfriends, and even more so after knowing how much they were enjoying themselves, when I was sacrificing my chunk of time with them. Within a few days I realized that this made me grumpy at the end of the day, as I wasn't taking care of myself, in the process of putting others' needs above mine. I would often snap at you and your granny, not knowing why. Soon it occurred to me. I came to discover the importance of being happy myself in order to give happiness to others.

There's nothing selfish in doing things for yourself first, if it means that you can give the best version of yourself to others by doing so. And yes, the thing about happiness is that the more you give, the more happiness multiplies. So well, feed yourself with little doses of joy and produce enough to share it with everyone around you. There's no harm in grabbing that last piece of cake sometimes! Dump that stupid guilt. A slice of self-love doesn't hurt anyone. As you stuff your face with the yummy cake, remember how blessed you are to relish this moment. Keep smiling my sunshine boy!

Love,
Ma

Cycling towards Independence

Dear Viv,

Today on August 15th, as we salute our national flag as a gesture of respect to the independence we achieved from the rule of the British government, I wonder what exactly it means to be independent. It took our country 190 years to finally achieve freedom and become independent.

Most humans normally become independent between the age of 18 to 25, although it is subjective to gender, circumstances, culture, and the background one belongs to.

I still remember the day you took your first wobbly steps, throwing your hands up in the air to show how you did not need to lean or hold onto any support to walk confidently. It was such a proud moment for us at home. Of course it wasn't something that was exceptional or unexpected. Most babies start walking at some point. But for us it was a feat that our child had achieved. And the fact that he could manage himself on his own was akin to a miracle! It's not surprising that a majority of parents feel the same way about their own child's milestones.

The Cambridge dictionary defines independence as *"the ability to live your life without being helped or influenced by other people."*

I already see you as independent to a large extent for the way you have been brought up. All those years that I was a weekend mom to you, when I was away from you working in another city, has helped you in many ways in becoming self-sufficient. I am glad this experience has molded you into a person who can find his way around most things with little help from others

Of course I always had one eye on you all through it. Distance did not matter. My daily conversations with you helped me figure out whether you were on the right track. And whenever I sensed your need for support, I left my work responsibilities to be with you. The guilt I would feel for the time that I was away from you, would slowly get replaced with the assurance of seeing you grow in a balanced manner, into an individual who required a balance of space and companionship.

However, the real test of your independence will be when you first step out of the house for your future education, all on your own in a new place. I gently leave you to soar high to explore the vastness of the world, holding onto the confidence I have in you.

You are indeed lucky to be able to be on your own at such a young age. Travel teaches you lessons that remain with you for life. It broadens your perspective of the world in a healthy way. It also teaches you to have your own thoughts and ideologies based on your own convictions, that need not necessarily conform to what other people think or believe.

In 2006 I had taken my first tentative steps towards independence. Unlike you, living on my own in a strange new city came to me quite late in life. Who would have thought that a woman who had never stepped out of her little town on her own would land up in an awe-inspiring city like Mumbai? And all alone too after becoming a mother? Well, some things are pure destiny. You know I had my reasons. Regardless of the reasons, I'm glad I had the chance to finally taste the true meaning of independence.

I remember being asked a question during the interview for the job assignment I had applied to. The head of Human Resources asked me if I was familiar with Mumbai since I was being considered for a role that required me to travel throughout the city on a regular basis. *"Are you familiar with Andheri?"* he asked me casually, *"And Bandra?"* he went on. I calmly answered, *"Not yet, but I'll soon figure it out."* Now when I look back, I think about how ridiculous it sounded for a person to not know the areas that were so popular in Mumbai, especially when being considered for a role that required them to travel within the city. I assume it was because of my confidence, despite my ignorance, that I landed the position.

I was doing things in Mumbai that I had never done before. Being overprotected prior, I never had a chance to do a lot of things. I recollect with amusement how I used to get my travel tickets to go home on weekends by post, all the way from our home at Baroda to Mumbai. Eventually I learned how to simply order my tickets online. I am sure you'll have your own first-timers and some years down the road, you will smile at the memories.

While you take your own responsibilities upon your young shoulders, remember that you will need to tread with caution and be aware of every action you take. This reminds me of the time when as a six-year-old you cycled all the way to your granny's place, a good six kilometers away from home without letting anybody know. While I was at work, your nanny was under the impression that you were playing with your friends outside the building, unaware of what you were actually up to. She only got to know that my little hero had reached his granny's place (cycling through the heavy main road traffic) when she telephoned the nanny to inform her about your brave adventure. We had to send the driver to fetch you and the bicycle back home safely in the car.

After your returned home, I gave you a sound scolding. I asked you, *"How on earth did you manage to cycle in such heavy traffic?!"* You shrugged your tiny shoulders and replied coolly, *"I cycled on the side of the road Mamma."* I must admit that while the very thought of you cycling on that road where heavy vehicles ply panicked me, a part of me was proud of your confidence in doing so!

I observe that most men believe they are independent, but ask them to cook a decent meal for the family or do the laundry, and you come to know how many are truly independent. Some men assume that earning a living is all they need to do which really is not a sign of an independent man. A man should be considered completely independent only when he stops depending on his mother, wife, sister, or housekeeper to do everything for him. That includes cooking, cleaning, and looking after all his needs besides going to work. The day you can fit into this bill is when I will proudly certify you as being truly independent.

For some time now, a harrowed mother has been checking with her son if he's carrying his wallet with him every time he leaves the house. It panics her to no end when he forgets to do so. He does not realize how such carelessness can turn into an ordeal, especially when you're in a new city. So my dear son, get some good habits into place before you go through some unwanted adventures in your future days of independence. Slip that wallet into your pocket now!

While a part of me yearns to keep doing things for you, I remind myself how long it took me to get to learn to do things on my own. That's why I step back and let you do your own things.

A lot of people tell me I'm brave to let my son go to a new place at such a young age, and that I should wait till he at least graduates before I could let him be on his own. But I know somewhere along the line, I would be restricting you if I hold you back. It would delay your independence.

I also know that if, as a six-year-old you had the sense to cycle on the side of the road, and possessed the bravery to do so in heavy traffic, then you'll be successful no matter what. In time you will also remember to carry your wallet without your mother's reminders!

Love,
Ma

Accepting Jealousy

Dear Viv,

Hope you've been enjoying all my letters so far. They might sound preachy, but well that's what mothers and teachers are famous for, aren't they? Anyway, I do hope these experiences and my own life lessons that I share with you, might help you in some way when you're looking for answers that elude you in sticky situations.

Today I want to write to you about the green monster otherwise known as jealousy, the one that exists to some extent in all of us and rears its ugly head in unflattering ways. It is a monstrous emotion that we become exposed to in a toxic way. Whether it is you who is jealous or it is someone else who is jealous of you, either way it isn't a pleasant situation. Let's accept that we are human, with each of us struggling with our shortcomings, yearning for things that we don't have, and wistfully watching others blessed with those things.

One of the first ways of coping with jealousy is being honest with oneself, without being in denial. A lot of us would never wish to acknowledge being jealous, for the fear of being judged.

The best way to identify jealousy is when you don't feel happy about someone else's happiness, especially if the reason for their happiness does not harm anyone. When you recognize this emotion within yourself, first sit and introspect as to what exactly about the situation is bothering you. Is it someone's new possession or privilege that's beyond your reach at this point? Is it your friend's hot new girlfriend? Or is it someone close giving your share of time to someone else?

Put yourself in the place of the person you feel is getting your share of the deal and analyze how you would feel if you had it for yourself. Truly believe that you do have it for yourself. Once you feel the comfort of owning what you think you want, ponder on how bad it would be if you let it go. You might say *"real bad."* I would say *"doable."*

Nevertheless, sometimes the thought of letting go of things is usually more difficult to handle than the actual process of letting things go. It is our mind that blocks us in such situations that does not allow us to let go. Once we know our mind better, it is easier to feed it with emotions that can help us overcome negative emotions and focusing on our positives. No matter how bad the situation is, avoid being competitive. Competition is beneficial when it's healthy. When competition breeds out of jealousy, it leads to many more ego and personality issues.

At the risk of sounding narcissist, I would like to share with you that I have come across more situations where I have found people to be jealous of me than me of them. I say this rather objectively without any illusions about myself or of others, after having judged many situations in an unbiased manner. While there are times that it has boosted my ego and self-image, there are other instances where I feel empathy towards another. This is because my intention is never to make someone feel bad about themselves. I strive to be the best version of myself, and if in that process it makes someone feel insecure or jealous, I somehow feel that I am instrumental in making them feel that way.

Owing to this, there have been situations where

I have gently raised it with people, especially close relationships by prodding them on how they feel about it. But well, based on my experiences, I can tell you that this kind of confrontation only works with people who are mature and secure in their skin. The ones who are not will deny and defend how they feel. But subtle signs especially in their body language and voice gives it away in many ways. Pay attention when people do not clap for your victories. They're often the ones who rush to you when you're in the dumps to offer you fake solicitude. However the moment you're in your element, they're not around.

Long time ago when buying a car was the luxury of a select few in India, one of our neighbors, the Kumars, had the privilege to buy one. Unfortunately for Mr. Kumar it was more of a necessity rather than a luxury, since his wife had suffered an accident. She had a weak back so was thus unable to ride in any other means of transport other than a four-wheeler. Other means were notorious for bumpy rides.

Somehow this new acquisition by the family was not well received by one of their neighbors, the Saxenas, who lived in the same building. They probably were unaware of the reason why the Kumars had to buy the car. To the utter shock of the entire neighborhood, one morning their new shiny car was found with leftover food thrown onto it from the balcony above. You guessed it right, the balcony belonged to the Saxenas. Mr. Kumar being the kind man that he was, initially assumed that it was an accident, that is, until it became a regular episode. On several occasions he would find eggshells and onion peels strewn on the car bonnet, and on other days it would be covered with bits of waste paper.

The Kumars ignored this for quite awhile, not wanting to get into any altercations with the Saxenas in order to maintain peace in their neighborhood. Unfortunately they could not find another place to park their car, since the building could not provide them with any other vacant parking place. This continued until Mr. Kumar found his car roof dripping with stale gravy thrown unceremoniously by the Saxenas.

After this particular incident, the Kumars confronted the Saxenas. Obviously the Saxenas denied the accusation and refused to admit that it was their doing. The fact that they did this out of jealousy was obvious. The society maintenance team was unable to help them since the Saxenas never admitted that it was their doing. Despite telling the Saxenas about Mrs. Kumar's health condition that required them to buy the car, it did not evoke any kind of empathy from the Saxenas who were on the defensive. After the confrontation, the car still received showers of mess, but the regularity had decreased. The Kumars knew better than to make an issue out of it. They would gently clean the mess and get on with their routine.

A few months later the Kumars were rudely awakened in the middle of the night. Someone was ringing on their doorbell incessantly. It turned out to be Mrs. Saxena. She was in a disheveled state and looked like she had seen a ghost. Mr. Saxena had suffered a stroke and the only people she could run for help were the Kumars. In the need of the hour, Mr. Kumar kept their differences aside and rushed Mr. Saxena to the nearest hospital in his car which saved his life. Since then, his car remains spotlessly clean every single day. It took a near-death situation for the Saxenas to do away with the toxic emotion of jealousy.

So, well, life is like that sometimes. No matter how positively you try to deal with a situation, you might not be able to see the results you want. Life has its ways of making people come to terms with their own issues when nothing else works. Until then, all one can do is stay positive without letting other people's insecurities affect you.

My suggestion to you regarding jealousy is to confront a person gently only if you feel it would help ease the situation. The way it will be received will vary depending on the person's nature and maturity. If you feel that confronting a person would not be a good idea, it is better to distance oneself from the person and situation for the time being. If it is meant to be, the person will sort their own feelings and get back to you when they are ready. If not, then it is best to accept that it's time to let it go. While empathy and kindness are important, nothing is more important than your own peace of mind.

All I can say is do not let emotions like jealousy make you feel good or bad about yourself. When you notice people being jealous of you, do not let it get to your head. It was most likely triggered due to a quality you possess that the other person does not. At the same time, remember that the emotion came from a place of distorted thinking, and hence should not be used as a parameter of judging oneself. I say distorted thinking because how is it possible that two people can have all the good qualities or luck? If a person is unable to accept that universal truth, their thinking is distorted. Same goes for when you feel jealous of someone. It can never be a parameter for judging yourself.

Each one of us is blessed with our own individual qualities, both good and bad. Acknowledge jealousy, work on it gently, and move forward. There are some emotions that help us evolve as humans. This is one of them.

Love,
Ma

Kindness and Gratitude

Dear Viv,

Ever since you were a little child, I observed that you were always generous by nature. In fact, there were times when I reprimanded you for blindly giving away things or doing favors for friends that never got reciprocated. I felt that the world would exploit this vulnerable quality of yours. I guess it was a maternal instinct of protecting you from being taken advantage of by others. Now that you're a grown-up, I think you should nurture this quality into something more meaningful.

In my previous letter, I spoke about kindness and empathy. There are certain emotions that serve to nourish your soul. Kindness and gratitude create positive vibrations around you. One can consciously practice these emotions until they become a natural part of our everyday lives.

Kindness is selfless and the gentlest of acts. When one is kind, it is easy to feel gratitude. Gratitude is a key characteristic of a kind person.

By now you're probably wondering why your mum is feeding you with so much philosophy. The reason I am writing to you about these qualities is that I know from personal experience that they create miracles if you adopt them in your daily life. They are powerful enough to come back to you in manifold ways. If you've heard the adage *"What you sow is what you reap,"* you would understand what I'm getting at.

A few years ago I attended an Art of Living workshop in Mumbai. The participants were asked to do at least one act of kindness each day, for the entire duration of the workshop which was about seven days.

Since I am an animal lover, the next day I went looking for stray dogs in the vicinity to feed. The following day our instructor asked us to do an act of kindness different from what we did the previous day. I did my bit by buying some coloring books from the kids at the traffic lights signal who sell it although I didn't really need them. The day after that I helped a colleague cope with her stress, by listening patiently to her and advising her on how to deal with it.

Each day I had to figure out various acts of kindness that I could do daily. I must say it wasn't easy to come up with so many random acts of kindness at all, because I hadn't really spared much thought to this in past. However, the joy of doing that exercise opened a new way of thinking for me. Slowly I began to be more observant on how people reacted to their surroundings and how it affected them.

A colleague of mine was known to be a shrewd person and had the reputation of being selfish. On one of my official tours with him, we happened to come across a famous temple. We decided to make a quick visit to offer our prayers. When we stepped out, we stopped by a food stall to grab something to eat. My colleague did something that took me completely by surprise.

As seen outside most Indian temples, there was a group of beggars who followed us for alms. When we were at the food stall serving *vada paav*, my colleague instructed the food hawker to serve the beggars with as many *vada-paavs* as they wanted. He also went ahead to tell them to call their other mates who were missing from the scene. Soon the bunch of six or seven turned into a large group of 25 to 30.

I had no words for my colleague's act. He was the last person I would have expected to do something generous like that. When I questioned him about it later, he replied saying, "*Dua lagti hai inki*," meaning "*their (beggars) prayers are blessings*." I was stumped by how simple his philosophy was. After witnessing this side of him, I quietly used to observe him doing the same for street urchins outside our office building. It is worth observing such people and imbibing good qualities from them.

Give as generously as you can to the needy, and in return they bless you by praying for you. By doing this you also express gratitude for being able to do so.

A few years ago I discovered the formal term used to describe this process. 'Tithing' is a way to bring God into our work and our relationship with money. To tithe means to give a certain amount of our income to God. Of course we can't give directly to God, so in practice we tithe to that which inspires us to draw closer to God. Tithe means "*one-tenth,*" so traditionally we give 10 percent, but in fact we can give any percentage we choose. Sometimes we need to start small until we can build up our faith.

Now you understand why we make those quiet trips to the local orphanage and old age homes. Have you noticed a sense of contentment you feel after sharing a bit of what you can with those deprived souls? You can also share your knowledge, volunteer free services, and offer small random acts of kindness to make someone's day. Once you experience the joy of giving, it grows on you, and gives you a sense of peace and joy that is beyond description.

By the way, have you ever heard the saying, *"Charity begins at home?"* How about offering to carry heavy shopping bags for your mum when we go shopping next? Nah, just kidding! On a serious note though, be aware of the needs of others. You will see a world of difference that you can make in the life of others. This, in turn, will add so much value to your own life. May the good you do to others come back to you in multiple ways, my dear child. God bless you!

Love,
Ma

Let's Talk about Love

Dear Viv,

This letter comes from someone who loved you even before you came into this world! So love is definitely an emotion that I want to write to you about.

I still remember the day the nurse brought your chubby little face in front of mine for the very first time. That moment of connection between us was magical. It seems to have gotten recorded vividly in my memory like a video. The look you gave me with your black beady eyes was that of a confused frown. I was amused to see the mix of emotions on your face. After that surge of maternal love within me, everything changed for me in that very moment. Ever since then no other love can replace the one that I have for you.

As you grow older you discover various shades of this emotion. You understand that the kind of love you share with your parents, grandparents, cousins, and other members of your family is different from the bond you have with your friends. All is good until it starts getting confusing when you become an adolescent. Gone are the days when you used to hate girls. Suddenly now you crave for their attention.

I am glad you're not one of those boys who would want to keep a girlfriend just so that you could flaunt her amongst your friends. A woman deserves much more respect than being treated as a trophy to be shown off.

There will be times when you wish for that one person who loves you and accepts you for who you are.

The experience of love is heavily laced with attraction, so in fact you might fool yourself into mistaking infatuation for love. Bear in mind that infatuation or attraction can happen instantly, whereas love takes time to grow. Love at first sight is another name for infatuation.

We've been talking about this for some time now, ever since you have grown to understand the dynamics of attraction. While you're too young to get into a serious relationship, at your age you should be focusing on meeting many types of people and understanding yourself better as a result. If you prefer to call it dating, that's fine. I would call dating as a time to get to know each other.

The love that you might wait for should come with understanding the person on a deeper level, rather than just superficial attraction that dies out even before you realize it. Sometimes the feelings that you have could be one-sided. Also, there could be times when either of you changes into different people and you no longer relate to each other. Do not let such experiences let you down.

I always go by the adage that unless you love yourself, you will not be able to love others. Understand that certain things are not meant to be. There is a larger picture to it. Someone far more interesting is waiting to appear in front of you to complete your life. Love is a beautiful emotion. Waiting for the right person is sure worth it!

You've been telling me that your first relationship will always be with someone you've been friends with. I respect the thought behind it. You're in an ideal situation then because you already know the person somewhat, before you venture into something deeper with them. However relationships are tricky. Sometimes you meet a person for the first time and you feel that you've known them for ages.

My friends Reshmi and Ayush were childhood friends. They were so close and attached to each other that they decided to tie the knot when they were of marriageable age. Their parents readily agreed to their decision, since they assumed that both of them were just right for each other.

Things were seemingly okay in the beginning, but a few years into their marriage boredom had set in. The attachment they had mistaken for love was slowly taking the brunt of overfamiliarity that resulted in a dull marriage. A few years down the road, Reshmi met a man at her workplace who she struck a chord with. The chemistry was instant. Suddenly she realized what had been missing in her marriage. She had an honest discussion with Ayush who understood her despite being disturbed by the turn of events. They got divorced on amicable grounds and Reshmi ended up marrying the guy she met. Within a few years Ayush met a charming woman through a friend, and now they are happily married. So, well, sometimes we make assumptions about love but end up getting surprises! That's how life is.

It is natural to develop feelings for someone you are fond of. At this stage I would urge you not to evaluate those feelings too much. This is the time to be carefree, to mingle, and first understand what you want from life. When you're busy discovering yourself, how would you have the clarity of what another person is all about?

Hence for the time being, enjoy the company of a wide range of people. Get to know them better. Find out what makes them tick. Does it excite you? Do your vibes match? Does she enjoy sharing a slice of pizza with you or is she the *dal-chawal* kind. Oh yes, these small things matter in the long run! In time you will know what you want from life, and from the person who deserves a special place in your life.

And when the time comes for that right person to walk into your life, keep this engraved in your mind and heart—this is from me:

Love will be like a flowing river. Do not expect it to gush with the same intensity as it started out with. In time it will calm down into a pool of placid waters. This period of placidity is mature love that transitions into mutual concern, with complete acceptance and assurance of what each of you means to each other.

Love,
Ma

To Be a Man

Dear Viv,

Hey, how're you doing young man? I've been reminiscing a lot lately about the years that have gone by. Time flies and how!

From the moment you crawled from my lap to toddle, and from the time you started to sprout stubble on your cheeks, I did not realize when my little boy became a man. There were times I wondered if the deep baritone of voice that you now talk in was a fake attempt at appearing older than your age. I guess at your age most boys want to look and sound a bit older to pass off as adults, and to get some added privileges like watching an adults-only movie!

However it's not such a cakewalk my son. No sir. There are certain prerequisites that you need to meet in order to qualify as a man. I'm not speaking about the natural ones that come with age, but the qualities within you that make you a man of character. As a woman, I can guide you on a few characteristics that could make you the kind of man people look up to. These traits probably don't match up to the ones that society has predetermined for you, but they sure will spruce you into a thorough gentleman.

You've had your share of pokes from me when it comes to chivalry. These are basic feel-good etiquettes according to me that express your concern to people around you, especially women. Holding the door for someone, speaking courteously over the phone (even with telecallers), giving up your seat on a crowded bus for senior citizens and people with disabilities, and women who are standing, are some common behaviors that show that you care to make people around you comfortable.

If I had a daughter, I would have told her the same thing. These qualities are not expected only in men. However they come naturally to most women due to their nurturing instincts. Men on the other hand need to learn these skills.

Being thoughtful has a lot to do with the way men have been raised and conditioned to treat women in a respectful way. This is partly due to the cultural values instilled in men that make them not act in accordance in a certain way. In some societies like ours, women do not command the kind of respect required for men to think about doing basic things for her to make her feel good about herself. After all the efforts a woman makes in different areas of life, be it bearing a child or taking care of their families, a little bit of extra concern can make tons of difference to their self-worth.

Most men assume that their only responsibility is to earn bread to provide for and protect their families. But what makes a 'real' man is when he can rise above the stereotypical persona of being a male chauvinist, and be sensitive, especially to the emotional needs of a woman.

One of our family friends, Shekhar, came from the traditional school of thought that women should only cook, clean, and take care of the children, while it was a man's prerogative to earn a living. I've seen his wife performing household chores even on days when she was ill. She was an educated lady who was capable of much more than household chores. But well, she could not venture out of the house due to her husband's narrow-minded outlook. The husband would never offer her help even when she was unwell. Not only that, but he also wouldn't offer to get her paid help or call in for food on such days.

Shekhar was a highly educated man with a decent job, but after a few years decided to start his own business which he was initially successful at. He even acquired his own office. However, somewhere along the line, he fell into a cycle of debt owing to miscalculated judgements. His business spiraled down and he ended up being sued by a lot of his clients to whom he owed a large number of debts. His property got sealed due to legal matters. His bad reputation followed him everywhere. People were not ready to employ him.

When things got out of hand, his wife stepped in. Despite her husband's reluctance, she took up a teaching job in the school where her son studied. She also pursued a correspondence course that further helped her qualify for better-paying work options. In the evenings, she started tutoring children who lived in the neighborhood.

Shekhar had no choice but to take care of the household responsibilities in her absence. Someone had to fill in the void. With time he started enjoying these chores, especially cooking. He realized how petty he had been all these years.

Today Shekhar runs a successful home-based business of making specialty bread. He nurtured his love for cooking by looking for recipes online and honing his skills. Thankfully he is out of debt now, and he enjoys his current profession which has given a new meaning to his life.

His wife continues her teaching job and the tuitions. Both of them share the household chores. Shekhar has learned to be respectful and empathetic to his wife's needs. His wife and kids adore his evolved thinking process.

Cooking, cleaning, and changing diapers does not make you any less of a man. Rather, to me, these are qualities I see in a man who has chosen to break the rigid mold that the patriarchal society has set him in. These are actually characteristics of an evolved man.

An evolved man is the kind of man who can accept the choices that a woman makes without dictating her on where and when she should go (or not go), whom she should mingle with, and how she should carry herself. He's the one who believes in letting people be who they are, by giving them the space and freedom that he craves for himself.

Standing up for women and protecting them comes as second-nature to most men. I'm sure you do not need my thoughts on that. Women these days are capable of taking care of themselves to a large extent. However, it gives them a sense of security when their man stands by them.

In the same manner in which society dictates how a man should leave a few chores for women, there are some behavioral dictates that are ridiculously targeted for men. For example, a man is not supposed to cry. I wonder how this theory came into being. That is how we all came into this world—bawling! So obviously it is a natural phenomenon that a man is asked to be deprived of. No wonder some women take advantage of this notion and shed tears at the slightest opportunity to get their way! So, no, a man who cries is real. He's not trying to be something that society wants him to conform to. He's man enough to be comfortable in his own skin to express what he feels, whether it is joy or sorrow.

Another theory is that a man is stronger than a woman. Physically, often, a man is stronger due to the way he is naturally built. But mentally a woman is much stronger than a man. I can count the mentally strong men I know on my fingers. They come by so rarely. The way your mind works, I can see a strong man emerging. Keep an open mind and trust me, someday you will make women in your life proud of you. This comes from one woman who is already proud of you, way too much, my precious man!

Love,
Ma

Learn to Say "No"

Dear Viv,

In one of my previous letters I had stressed the importance of kindness. But oftentimes we end up being hard on ourselves. How many times have you stopped to think if you're being kind to yourself? I bet not many.

In our bid to be accepted, we end up doing things that we are not happy doing, without resisting or protesting. There's this fear that we would be judged if we refused to comply. In turn we end up fitting into somebody else's plan without really wanting to. Someone may have managed to push us into doing something, without us wanting to do it in the first place!

Remember the last time you were unable to say no to someone? While you would have liked to say *"no,"* you mouthed a *"yes"* unsure on how to scoot out of the situation. Saying that yes made you uncomfortable about the situation.

There have been many such occasions when you have been invited to stay overnight at your friend's place after a long day. You would have loved to sleep off the day's exhaustion, but your friends insisted that you join them. You knew fully well that you'd be groggy the next day at school, and might end up getting sick after staying up late with your friends the night before.

Saying *"no"* and sticking to that would have avoided you the trouble, but you did not want to let your friends down. In this case, since it was an activity you enjoyed doing with your friends despite the lack of sleep, it wasn't that big a deal.

Later in life, when you rely heavily on time management (which is a much-needed skill in today's fast-paced world), you will need to prioritize your tasks in an effective manner.

Saying *"yes"* when you'd rather say *"no"* could put you in a disadvantageous position, especially in a professional scenario. Some people are always on the lookout for someone who cannot say *"no."* They have the knack of working on your guilt to get their task done. Pay close attention and recognize this pattern when someone does it time and again with you. Say *"no"* to them calmly but firmly. You are not being rude by saying *"no"* to something that causes you inconvenience or doesn't agree with you. It only highlights your assertiveness. When you learn to do this without any awkwardness or guilt, a person will think twice before making a request that is not agreeable with you.

Back in my college days one of my friends, Rahul, was trapped in such a situation. His girlfriend Saba would ask him to help her finish her submissions for her college assignments. Although it was apparent that he himself had a lot on his plate, she would insist on his help and he would comply without uttering a word. We would often wonder why he wouldn't put his foot down and tell her that he had his own assignments to finish.

At the end of the year Saba scored high marks for her work, whereas Rahul suffered badly in his own submissions. It did not end at that. This was a case of love being blind, deaf, and definitely dumb. He continued getting exploited by her without ever having a frank conversation with her, with the hope of settling down with her eventually. He probably said *"yes"* to everything she wanted him to do in spite of not wanting to, with the hope that she would say *"yes"* to his proposal for marriage someday. However once they graduated from college, the girl coolly walked away without any regret, while my friend was left nursing his broken heart and the frustration of being taken advantage of.

So, well, the world can be a bad place if you allow it to be. It has a fair share of manipulators who are on the prowl for someone who cannot say *"no."* Identify people who push your buttons and expect you to say *"yes"* all the time. It isn't that difficult really. When these things happen, your mind sends out signals of protest or displeasure. Listen to it. Do yourself a favor. Smile at the person and simply say *"no."*

Love,
Ma

An Ode to Obsession

Dear Viv,

Today I'm in the mood to talk about a quality that could be either good or bad depending on the situation—obsession.

Each one of us has our own set of obsessions. Be it giving into the temptations of the sweet tooth, to achieving the perfect body weight, or to scoring a certain percentage of marks, we all have something that obsesses us to no end.

An appropriate amount of preoccupation with the 'right' things is healthy and adds zest to our lives. It fuels our passion with a spark that ignites our being with a sense of purpose. People who lack the kind of obsession that fires their spirit are often seen as dull and uninterested about life in general. On one hand, I feel sympathetic towards such people for their lack of drive, but on the other hand, I sometimes lose my patience with them for their inability to even acknowledge it as a void in their lives.

And then there are people who fixate over the wrong things. For example, today social media is a raging craze. I think this medium gives people inappropriate opportunities to obsessively stalk, judge and troll people without guilt. Look at the number of cases on a rise nowadays, where celebrities have been mercilessly trolled on the internet. People take advantage of hiding behind a mask of anonymity, to churn out the most toxic kind of comments.

While very few of us seem to be able escape this obsession, the real concern is for people who have replaced their real life with living in their virtual lives 24/7. The drive for more important matters that add value to their lives, has been replaced with a screen that flashes updates on who is doing what and how many people acknowledge them in the virtual world.

Another habit that turns me off is when people feel the need to nitpick all the time. At the root of this persistent fault-finding is a pessimistic mind. If you ever come across people like this, treat them as though they have been infected. It is like a disease of the mind. Do not attempt to correct them or show them who they are. Ultimately it is their fixation whether they know it or not. Instead focus your interests on people, places, and topics that intrigue you in a good way, helping you learn and imagine new possibilities.

Sometimes I come across inspiring personalities that make me sit up and take notice. They have helped me decide on the qualities I wish to adapt from them. Some of them have been people I've known personally, while others I've observed as public figures. With those I have known personally, I often had long conversations and debates with them in order to understand them better. Those discussions have quenched my obsession of digging deep into the minds of people who think differently from me, so that I do not remain stagnant in my thought processes.

One of these, a friend's father was someone who gave up his religion completely and called himself a Marxist. My debates with him were often spiked with the religious ideologies I was brought up with. However, coming to understand his thoughts on the subject helped me move away from my own mindset for awhile, and analyze the subject from a neutral perspective.

Yet another person I am absolutely curious about is a close friend of your granny. I haven't met her in person but I have had to the chance to connect with her over social media. She happens to be someone who claims to receive messages through musical notes. She intuits outcomes based on those messages, and surprisingly some of it has come true for me. The mystical quality in her intrigues me to learn more about her gift.

And then there are some public figures that I have been following closely with, in the way they have aged gracefully in thought, action, and personality. Obsessing over the admirable qualities of some of these personalities have helped me shape into who I am today.

Thankfully I have been blessed with a son like you, who shows a healthy interest in subjects that make him curious. It is one of your best qualities. Your love affair with books makes me proud. The fact that you try to get your hand on the next book you plan to read (even before you end the book you've been reading), is a trait that has helped you in the best of ways

Let your list of healthy obsessions grow to help you evolve to a multifaceted personality with interesting perspectives. And hopefully someday, you will be on the list of people who obsess to learn from you and be like you—priceless!

Love,
Ma

Fruits of Patience

Dear Viv,

In the last few days I have sat with you at unearthly hours. Your eyes were glued to the hands of the clock as each second ticked by, while you kept refreshing the page on your laptop. It would soon announce your acceptance or rejection in the university you applied to. Those seconds that ticked by dragged each ounce of our patience with mixed feelings of hope and trepidation.

Life is like that. When you want something badly, it seems to take forever. The wait for it tests us in various ways. How desperately you want something is what decides your level of patience for its result. You will be thrown in such situations often when your patience will be put to the test. How calm you keep yourself during these crucial waiting periods, determines how you will face the outcome.

People generally pace and fidget at such times, causing upheaval for people around them. Their anxiety levels shoot up and they behave as though their life depends on that one thing they are waiting for. And supposing the end result of the wait is the opposite of what they wanted, the dams of their bridled patience bursts in an instant.

I have always admired people who remain cool, calm, and collected in the face of such crucial seconds. I've had the chance to speak to such people to know how they keep their patience at bay. One person shared that their trick has been to think of alternatives they could resort to, if the desired outcome did not come through. This helped their mind focus on a larger perspective than just that one single result that they desired. Besides distracting the mind from negative thoughts, this technique helped them improve their patience.

No matter how badly you want something to happen, sometimes there are ways of getting there if you could not reach there by the straight route. These alternative routes might take time, but with sheer patience and calculated efforts, nothing is impossible. That's the reason why they say that there is no shortcut to success. Life doesn't always follow a straight line, there are usually zigzag patterns!

If you recall, I shared my personal experiences of my professional journey with you in one of my previous letters. I refused to take my limitations as roadblocks to get to where I wanted to go. I am not exactly the most patient person, though I did persist and put in the effort to see the culminated result at the end of a good 22 years. I have shared this as an example to you on numerous occasions, when you have expressed your wish to follow the dream of an unconventional profession. If I can do it, so can you!

I admire your courage in deciding to go for your dreams and pray that you reach great heights as you make each of them come true. However, from my own experience and knowing how this world functions, it requires a safety net of income to first feel secure before moving towards the passion that you've put your heart into. Being practical and patient is important, and even more so when you are being brave enough to tread the unconventional path. Study your options, plan well, and have a backup plan. Put in consistent effort, and last but not least, give time and patience to watch your dreams turn into reality.

Love,
Ma

Quitting the Quest

Dear Viv,

As you're certainly aware, it's been close to six months since I started going for daily walks. I did this to shed some of the extra pounds that I had accumulated. I installed a fitness App on my cellphone to monitor my progress. Initially I started taking walks in a park close by with a friend for about half an hour every day. Within a few days, my friend could not remain committed to the routine. However I was seeing progress in my weight loss already, so I stuck to my routine.

In fact I challenged myself a little more, bit by bit, day by day. From a modest 3,500 steps a day, I increased to 5,000 and then 10,000 steps within the span of a few weeks. I would put on my headphones and sweat during my walkathons. My major motivation was inch loss and lesser numbers showing on my weighing scale. However, as of late, despite the constantly fulfilling results, I find this routine monotonous. It's something that I can do effortlessly without putting in too much thought or energy. I guess I need to find another form of working out to challenge my faculties further.

Oftentimes our lives start feeling dreary. We go about our routines mechanically, doing our tasks mindlessly. We're probably stagnating, but yet we carry on without bothering to make changes in our lifestyle. I've observed the sharpest of minds going numb in the confinement of mundane routine. It is a sheer waste of mental resources when one goes into this kind of shell.

It is said that the mind needs to be challenged on a regular basis to keep it sharp and productive. Finding new pursuits that require the brain to make an extra effort to absorb new information, keeps the mind healthy and away from monotony.

For years we continue having the same interests, assuming that we know what we enjoy doing the most, without the will to try new things. Sometimes we get plain lazy in our comfort zone to go that extra mile to chase a new quest. Or perhaps that particular activity does not seem to be what we are cut out for. Maybe it requires certain skills and stamina which we assume that we lack. We may be pushed into doing something out of courtesy to someone or to keep them company, and then discover to our surprise that we actually enjoy it! That happens a lot, doesn't it? But then why do we wait for some instance like that to oil our rusty minds?

Games and puzzles have been designed to keep our minds working in challenge mode. Remember all those games you played when you were a kid? Have you ever wondered when and why you stopped playing those games or reduced the frequency of playing them? Probably the day you started assuming that you're too old to play such seemingly frivolous games. That childlike wonder of discovering a new way of building blocks is replaced with a been-there-done-that or a not-interested mentality that does no good to your spirit.

No matter how old you are, keep that childlike quality of chasing new adventures to feed your mind with new matter, just the way you satiate your tongue with new tastes to bring in novelty. I say 'childlike' because being childlike is different from being 'childish.' A child has the most innocent form of curiosity. However as you grow older, you usually try to dim this curiosity within yourself by assuming to be plagued by boredom. You suddenly don't have time for these little explorations. But somewhere your mind rebels because it gets worn out by the mechanical format of working day in and day out without any new challenges. And then one day something within us dies. Life no longer seems as exciting as it used to be. Obviously it's because we ourselves have quit our quest to make life exciting.

If you ask me how you could continue chasing new challenges to conquer, I'd say try new things every once in awhile, even if they seem remotely interesting. Sometimes you end up surprising yourself by doing something that you probably never thought was possible and enjoying it.

For example, never in my wildest dreams did I ever imagine that I would one day bake cupcakes for you. I was always the type of cook who would get into the kitchen, rustle up something quickly, and get out of the kitchen. As a child when you would request me to make a particular dish that involved a complicated recipe, I would cheekily tell you that certain dishes are never made at home—they needed to be ordered from a restaurant! But one day my sweet tooth started to crave for something that I did not feel like ordering from outside. I finally ventured to do the very thing that I had labeled as too much effort and no fun.

I never thought that the acts of sieving flour, beating eggs, and whipping up a rich frosting would give me so much pleasure. In spite of all the effort, the heady aroma of vanilla essence wafting from the oven turned out to be very therapeutic for me. I graduated from baking cupcakes to making bread, trying to learn new skills by looking up recipes on the internet. Today I'm glad I made that extra effort to break out of a mental block, that prevented me from trying something new. That also meant that you no longer could be fooled by being told that certain things are never made at home! So, well, you can now have your cake and eat it too!

In the end, all I can say is keep the pursuit for new things alive to enrich your life. Quitting is for losers. To reap the bounty that life has yet to bless us with, we need to put in consistent effort, and constantly work around our fixed mindsets to break out of the monotony that we have created for ourselves. I'd love to see what your next quest is going to be all about. C'mon, surprise me!

Love,
Ma

Rooting for Respect

Dear Viv,

How's it going? I hope you're enjoying these letters. Feel free to discuss or debate with me on anything that I write to you about if you have a different perspective. You need not take every word I write here as the final word out of respect for me. That brings me to one of my favorite topics—respect.

Recently someone paid me a compliment. He told me that I am a good human being, but he added that the only flaw I had was that I could not handle disrespect. He was right. However, it set me thinking on how that could be a flaw. Why would or why should anyone tolerate disrespect? After all, we humans thrive on admiration and acceptance from others.

Mutual respect is an unwritten rule of conduct that one should ideally follow. While it is important to give respect, one should strive to command respect. Using force or power to command respect is a sign of a weak person. If you ever find yourself in a situation where someone tries to extract respect out of you by undue means, do not hesitate to put your foot down. You need not rebel, but gently make it clear that you cannot be forced into something that doesn't come to you naturally. The right people will understand your concern and respect you for being honest about it.

To command respect, one needs to be humble and respectful themselves.

Surprisingly, it is observed that middle management employees are the ones who seem to be the most arrogant and overbearing. I've witnessed executive management employees in many organizations that I have worked with to be the humblest of all. These are the cream of top management, that is, CEOs and directors of companies who have worked their way up to the top. One CEO of a famous luxury brand of clothing, once helped to wash the floors of their new store that was about to be opened the following day. It so happened that on that particular day they had a shortage of staff. The CEO did not think twice about rolling up his sleeves, and got to work immediately with his team to get the store ready in time. To this day his staff hold him in high regard for his down-to-earth attitude, and quote his exemplary behavior in the industry.

As a baby when you started mumbling your first words, your Dad and I decided to address you as *'aap'* (you) in Hindi. This is a respectful way of addressing someone as opposed to '*tu*' (you) which we normally use to address people younger than us or of the same age. Since there is no such differentiation in the English language, when we say 'you,' in English it doesn't really matter who you're addressing. However in Indian vernacular languages, we really should be careful when it comes to how we address people of different ages. The wrong usage of pronoun indicates disrespect to the person whom it is directed towards and also sounds rude.

Although technically we should have called you *'tu,'* we decided otherwise so that you would learn to be respectful while talking to us. After all, we would have been the first ones you would have interacted with. As you grew up, you automatically developed the habit of addressing all elders as *'aap,'* irrespective of whether they were your parents, grandparents, or domestic helpers in our house.

To me holding that amount of respect for everyone matters, irrespective of their economic status, education, or age. It speaks of fine upbringing. I am confident that I have not gone wrong with it, especially now when I see you interacting with people of different ages and from different walks of life. It is said that if you ever want to judge a person's character, observe their behavior towards people who are not their equals.

It is commonly observed in our culture, that the kind of reverence a man gives to his own mother, sisters, and other female blood relatives is not given to other women he comes across in society, including his own wife. Behavioral traits are often learned from the elders in the family. For example, if the father does not treat his wife well, perhaps the son emulates the same. And that leads to a tilt in the balance of how a man treats women who don't belong to his immediate family.

A few months ago, in relation to this topic, I had said categorically that if ever I see you treating any woman with disrespect, I would extend all my support to that woman no matter what. That's how strongly I feel about treating women with respect.

As my child I expect you to respect everyone—man, woman, and child—irrespective of gender, caste, color, or economic status. However, a woman needs extra honor for the fact that she spends her entire life serving others. Each of us owes them that much for giving birth to us, raising us, and ensuring that we've reached this far.

Anyone who disrespects a woman loses my regard for them instantly, no matter the reasons for doing so. I am absolutely intolerant to disrespect. I guess this attitude of mine does not go down well with some men, since they may be used to women succumbing to disrespect in dire circumstances. That explains why the man who complimented me thought of it as a flaw.

The best way to show respect to a woman is by giving her the freedom to decide what she wants to do with herself, what she wants to wear, and how she wishes to lead her life. Respect her choices and you will command deep respect in return. That has been the way I have raised you as well.

I have always stood by you in your decisions and supported you, no matter how different it was from my own thought processes. This kind of acceptance of an individual is the ultimate respect that one can offer. I hope you take a cue and use this piece of ideology in your future interactions to gain the respect that you give others.

Love,
Ma

Success

Dear Viv,

The other day our neighbor Mrs. Shah came over with a box of sweets to celebrate her son's admission in a prestigious university. She was beaming with pride and happiness. I was truly happy for her, until I learned that her son had not secured the admission based on his merits.

They had actually paid a hefty donation to get him a seat in that university which the mother announced rather boastfully. I was disappointed, not for her son, but for the other deserving candidates who lost the chance of securing a seat in that university based on their hard-earned merits. Isn't it a sad state of affairs that our idea of success has become so distorted these days?

Like every mother on this earth, I want my son to be successful. I wish that he goes places and does things that make me proud. This does not necessarily mean earning fame and wealth. Although some amount of recognition and comforts are always welcome, those are not the only parameters of achieving success.

To me success comes slowly and steadily as you work towards bringing out the best version of yourself. It appears when you first evolve from the person who has set out to find yourself, to the person you discover along the way, digging in deeper for exploring your strengths and overcoming weaknesses.

Work is only one avenue where we achieve accolades, but a vocation should not be the only definition of success. Our values, thoughts, and actions also speak for how successful we've been in honing our personality. I see a lot of people around me who assume that their ultimate ambition in life is to acquire at least one degree from a prestigious university. Then they yearn to earn loads of money by either grabbing a well-paying job or by starting and expanding a business that may not require rocket science in running it. And that's success to them.

I believe that even after we step out of college, our learning does not stop there nor should it. Our curiosity should have us strive to continue learning. Success is beyond what we read in books. When we scratch the surface of information to explore the deep layers beneath is when we experience the true taste of success. Remember the sense of fulfillment that you feel when you've written a piece of an essay or shot a certain film clip, no matter how inconsequential it is? That contentment is what defines our personal triumphs. The moment when you pat yourself on the back is a moment of personal success. That absolute glee of discovering or creating something is immeasurable.

It is an unsaid unspoken rule in this world that you're only successful if you have high educational qualifications, wealth, and fame. Or, maybe if you speak good English! Yes, doesn't that sound ridiculous?! I mean, how can a lack of knowledge of a particular language be the criteria for deciding a person's intelligence and caliber?

I have come across illiterate people who happen to be much more intelligent and insightful as compared to some of the most highly educated people. They are self-taught individuals who use their eyes, hands, and minds to explore, observe, and innovate. They might have never referred to a book, but their practical experience and hands-on exposure is far richer than the knowledge available in books.

Our current Prime Minister, Narendra Modi, once sold tea at a roadside stall. Despite his humble roots, he has been able to reach a pinnacle of success, because he found a way to utilize his strengths and bring out the best version of himself. As a result, he is now leading our country to a new pathway of success under his able leadership.

Such people are exemplary visionaries who did not achieve success by rote. Along with a keen interest in finding answers, their persistence in following their passion is what makes them stand apart.

I am glad you have opted for a career that will give you the flexibility to explore and innovate. Make the most of it. However, do not get into the rut of not thinking beyond your career. Take a keen interest in varied topics. Read as much as you can, but more importantly, try to get practical experience which will give you a far richer bank of knowledge to carry with you.

There is a reason why people say that the more you travel, the wiser you become. The things you see, explore, and experience can take you places that confining yourself to a closed methodology of learning can never take you. So my dear, the world is your oyster. Swim the depths, soar the heights, and do so with your binoculars perched on!

To your success!

Love,
Ma

Building Integrity on Trust

Dear Viv,

I meant to write to you about integrity earlier, but I missed doing so in my previous letters. Since integrity is so closely related to trust, I thought it would make sense to write to you about how integrity can instill trust in people.

Your integrity is based on the balance of your actions and your words. We often hear people making tall claims about their high standards of thinking. However, when you observe them closely, very few of them actually supplement their actions in sync with their thoughts. This, in turn, shakes the trust that they had inculcated in people with thoughts that were not really theirs, but carefully crafted ones that would leave a favorable impression.

As the famous quote says:

Integrity is doing the right thing even when no one is watching.

It takes only an instant to win or break someone's trust, though it takes a lifetime to earn the legacy of integrity. Therefore be extremely cautious that your words and actions are in sync, so that you avoid breaking another's trust.

It is okay to be honest without sounding great. One does not need the mask of being a great human being to prove one's worth. Honesty is a much sought-after virtue in today's world. Not many people have the courage to own up to their true thoughts and feelings. But those who do, win the trust of others around them, because they show their true self to the world without leading others on.

The only flip side could be that some people who do not approve of your honest thoughts might reject them. They will however, appreciate you for coming clean with them. In any case you can never impress everyone all the time. If you attempt to do so, you will end up being dishonest with them and ultimately to yourself. Most people-pleasers remain so only for a brief while because very soon their masks fall off. They can't don multiple masks at the same time, and in no time people realize that they aren't who they truly show themselves to be.

When we're young we have this strong urge to be accepted by our peers. We go to great lengths to conform to their standards in order to fit in. It happens naturally as a part of growing up. Somewhere along the way we discover that we have our own likes and dislikes, which may not conform to someone else's. Being open about our individual likes and dislikes, without worrying too much about how it will be accepted, builds on your credibility. A transparent person is easy to trust.

As you go forward in life, there will be give-and-take relationships where extra effort is required to establish trust. This will be especially true for close friendships, relationships, and business partners.

People can mistrust your best intentions even when you are being open and truthful. This happens due to a person's own insecurities and sometimes due to misunderstandings. It would be sensible to have an open discussion in such situations to clear the air.

Certain people are naturally distrustful of others. It might be because of their own life experiences or upbringing that has caused them to be that way. It is advisable to tread softly around such people, to avoid getting yourself tangled in their drama. Understand that it is their problem, and stay away from situations where you could see yourself having issues with them.

When it comes to trusting other people, I believe you should give everyone a fair chance, though it is always a good idea to buy some time before you trust them completely. Get to know them better. Observe how they react in certain circumstances. Take non-verbal cues on deciding if the person is worthy of your trust or not.

For example, if you are to strike a partnership in a new venture with someone and you meet them for the first time, say in a restaurant, he might appear polite and easy to work with. But if you observe how he talks to a subordinate on the phone, or how he keeps recalculating the check that comes in after you've had your meal, you would definitely get an idea on the side of his true personality. This is the side that he doesn't prefer to show but unwittingly gives away, hoping that you have not noticed.

Do you remember the times I met some of your friends and formed an impression about them even without talking to them? Sometimes I have been pretty on the mark on my observations about them which you yourself confirmed later. These observations come from years of practice in closely observing human behavior. Most of my observations have been tried, tested, and authenticated with real life experiences. Some learnings are still in process and await validation.

As a visual merchandiser when I had to interview a candidate on my team, I would casually skim my eyes on their fingers and toenails. The way their nails were maintained was a clear giveaway on how honest the candidate was. After all visual merchandising is all about effective presentation. The question is, if a person cannot present themselves in a proper manner, addressing finer details, how could they help me set up my stores in an organized manner? No matter how smooth they might talk, it might not match their actions when they get on the job if they're sloppy with presenting themselves!

Again, winning trust is as important as placing trust in people. Hold on tight to the ones who have proved their trust in you and trust you in equal measure. They are difficult to come by. Someday I hope to know from people that my son is someone they trust with all their heart, due to the integrity that he has carefully carved for himself. I have complete trust in you, *Beta*. I wish you all the best.

Love,
Ma

Unique You

Dear Viv,

Before you were born, I would often imagine what kind of baby you would turn out to be. I fantasized that you would be one of a kind, unique and unlike any other child. The most special child in the world.

I wanted my child to be an individual in his own right. I guess all parents dream about this for their child. No wonder we go about choosing unique names for our children selecting the best of the things that we could offer them. That includes education, comforts, and values, each personalized to shape their child into an original personality that parents could be proud of in the days to come.

Back then, when we named you, your name was unique and unheard of. Besides being an amalgamation of the first two letters of your parents' names, it also has a beautiful meaning. Your name means 'fresh flowers' in the Konkani language. It truly denotes what your parents wanted you to be—fresh and unique like a newly bloomed flower, with interesting shapes to each petal, and a fragrance that would fill our lives with bliss.

You did not disappoint us at all. You are every bit as unique as I had hoped you to be, or maybe a little more than that. It could be a mother's pride that's making me say this, but I notice that appreciation in the eyes of every person who knows you for who you are.

So probably I am not being delusional out of blinded maternal love.

As your parents, while we acknowledge and feel blessed about your uniqueness, let us also accept that God has made you different, in the same way that God has attributed unique qualities in each person. No matter how different or better we find ourselves in comparison to others, everyone is blessed with their own unique qualities.

Therefore, always be grateful for the blessings that God has showered upon you. At the same time, be humble enough to appreciate and acknowledge the good in others. Train yourself to spot good qualities in a person when you interact with them. Being inspired by others can help to hone qualities within you.

You might also notice some bad traits within another, but choose to focus on the good ones to make the most out of your interactions with them. Sometimes when you know how good you are, it could lead to an inflated ego if not kept under check. The practice of seeing the positive characteristics in others, also helps keep arrogance and false pride at bay.

Another thing to remember when it comes to being original is to not be fazed by what people think about you. You're born to be different. If you change yourself only to fit into a certain mold that society expects of you, you lose out on the opportunity to be yourself. Being yourself is the biggest gift you can give yourself. Nothing is more refreshing than interacting with an individual who does not need to slip behind a facade to impress. A person who is comfortable in their own skin, taking their imperfections in stride, comes across as a confident individual.

While I was growing up and transitioning into a mature adult, I adapted a few time-tested methods that helped me remain true to who I was. I still try and stick by these principles. They do not let me get lost in the maze of identical thought processes and personalities that a majority of people follow. This herd mentality not only stops me from being analytical, but is also quite restrictive in approach when we adapt it according to our own individual personalities. Here are a few things I swear by when it comes to being my own person:

1. Let no one tell you that you're too old to do something. If you feel like floating paper boats in puddles, do so without giving a second thought to what people think about you.
2. You are the one who decides your own likes and dislikes. Just because what you admire is not accepted by your friend does not mean that it is not worthy of being liked and likewise. Likes and dislikes are subjective and cannot be generic ever.
3. Do not get into the 'trend-slave' mode. Being updated with new trends may be okay; however, if you have to bend over backwards to adapt to a trend, it really will not help you to be yourself. What you wear should be effortless yet smart on you, be it a hairstyle, your clothes, or your attitude. Keep it simple and smooth.
4. Do not process any information based on hearsay. Use your logic and intuition to build your opinions based on your own understanding of the information. You have a right to hold onto your perspective.
5. Keep learning. The more you learn, the more you evolve. Your lessons are great deciding factors in how different you are from others.
6. Do not feel ashamed or guilty if your thoughts on a certain topic are different from others. Your opinions are like your signature: unique.

7. Last but not least, be proud of who you are, no matter what you look like, what your background is, or what your academic/professional/economic standing in society is. Avoid succumbing to ridicule, scorn, and unjust criticism. Wear your individuality on your sleeve with your head held high.

Most of the above-mentioned traits have helped me be myself through my ups and downs. Situations and circumstances changed, so did I, but only to improvise myself on what I was yesterday without changing the core personality of who I really am.

From a young age, you've been your own person too. While I debated with you on your views of religion, I admired you for having the nerve to analyze and have an opinion just the same. Most kids would blindly follow things like religion and traditions, but not you. No matter how much I desire that you follow the values that we as parents have instilled in you, I would still expect that you use your fair judgment in every sphere of your life to be true to yourself.

So while you're out there, do retain your original flavor as you assimilate a whole lot of new learnings that will only add to your uniqueness. Be good. Be you!

Love,
Ma

The Value of Life

Dear Viv,

Today let's talk about life. Our life is the dearest thing we hold onto. Somewhere our attachment to life is where all our fears come from. We fear losing our life. We fear being unsuccessful in life. We fear being unhappy in life. We fear being lonely in life. The list goes on and on, and the word 'fear' always has to do with something not going right in our lives.

That brings me to the question: Why do we value our lives so much? I tried to find the answer to it and here's what I came up with. From the moment we are born, we are thrown into a vacuum of the unknown. We do not know what is coming next. When we open our beady eyes to this new world, we start wondering what's going to happen next.

After you were born, little did you know that the shiny object that missed your eye was actually a pair of scissors. The nurse lifted you up and snipped off the umbilical cord that was your only connection with your mother. Ouch! Had you known, you might have done something about it. Wailed harder maybe!

Who would have wanted to go into this big crazy world had they known what it entailed? It would have been so much cozier to confine yourself to the familiar warmth of your mother, right? But well, it was too late by then. And thereafter starts this cycle of not knowing what to expect next. Although it sounds adventurous to head towards the unknown, you don't feel much in control due to the uncertainty of it all. Each new step you take may be accompanied with the fear of falling, but somewhere along the way you accept it as a way of life. However, it leaves you teaching the vital lesson of respecting and valuing your life.

While we all know that life comes with an expiry date, very few of us try to make the most of it. We whine about little things. We focus on issues that do not go right. We do all the wrong things to ourselves and go about trying to make our own living hell. When we know how valuable life is, why don't we take extra effort to care for it? You may wonder how.

Well, have you realized that most of us do not start taking precautionary measures until a crisis strikes? We often do not start studying until we score less on our exams. We do not eat healthy, exercise, and meditate till it starts showing on our bodies and on our stress levels. We do not have protected sex, in spite of knowing the hazards of sexually transmitted diseases and unwanted pregnancies.We do not drive safe until we end up in an accident due to reckless driving.

Yet we fool ourselves believing that we value our lives. We blindly assume that we value our lives. Not many of us seem to. We go about making the same blunders again and again until life suddenly hits us hard to remind us how fragile it really is.

I have a friend who once was a biker. He had a passion for riding his mean machine for long stretches through different terrains at precarious speeds. Many people advised him to keep a check on that; however he wouldn't heed them. He had won several medals for covering difficult paths in the shortest amount of time, breaking a lot of records, and that gave him an adrenaline rush that was incomparable.

On one expedition, he was maneuvering his way through particularly mountainous terrain and it was drizzling that day. He lost control and skidded down the road into a gorge, plunging into a 50-foot valley.

Thankfully he was saved and rescued by local villagers. He narrowly missed losing his life and ended up with innumerable fractures and injuries that crippled him for life. That was the last time he ever rode his bike. Now he knows the value of his life.

After his recovery, he was forbidden from riding. He nurtured an interest in nature photography and developed this newfound passion. If only he had restrained his speeding he would have been able to continue biking. However, that incident turned his life around, and he now understands how precious life is.

There are a number of things that I have set as priorities to help me value my life better. I hope you can refer to these and make a set of your own.

1. Live in the moment, but do not let it spoil the days to come.
2. Do not throw your life away for one person or situation. There's a whole new world out there to explore. Value your life enough to acknowledge that.
3. Do tiny favors for your body. Balance binge eating with some physical activity/exercise or compensating for it by eating healthy meals that follow.
4. Learn basic skills like cooking, driving, swimming, banking, and sewing buttons.
5. Be aware of your physical surroundings. Keep yourself updated on what is happening around you. Catch up on the daily news. Whether you're driving on the roads or relaxing on your bed, being alert

can save you from the worst of the calamities that can strike any moment.

6. Look up random things that you do not know about for no reason. You never know when they could be useful.
7. Be flexible. I often tell fussy eaters to imagine what they would do if there's a world war and they land as refugees in a foreign country, that does not provide them the kind of food they are accustomed to eating.
8. Do at least one activity a day that makes you feel productive. It could be as simple as watering the plants or offering help to someone.
9. Have at least one interest that soothes your senses. It could be listening to music or writing a journal.
10. Surround yourself with optimistic people who enrich your life.

I could go on with this list adding more to it along the journey of life. After all, life is valuable. I intend to make the most of it and so should you. Always remember that your life is as precious to me as it is to you. Live it to the fullest with your mind, body, and soul in sync as best you can. Live life king-size!

Love,
Ma

The Wealth of Wellness

Dear Viv,

You've known your mother as a fairly disciplined person when it comes to wellness and health. While I am a partner in crime the day you wish to dig into a box of creamy doughnuts, or help you to finish the last bite of a burger, there are days that you've seen me drawing the line.

All these years saw me monitoring your diet and other activities to keep your lifestyle balanced and healthy. A few months from now, you will solely be in charge of your well-being. When you start living by yourself you may tend to slip in a devil-may-care attitude when it comes to eating healthy food and getting enough rest. Feeling high on the rush of a new adventure, you might push healthy self-care at the back of your priority list. I am sure that you won't go hungry being a 'foodie.' My concern, however, is your love for rich food that you tend to indulge in.

We both share a common love for exploring different kinds of foodstuff, but knowing how overindulgence acts on the body in the long run, has kept me balanced in terms of knowing when to stop. While I do not claim to be the healthiest person with the fittest body, a few ground rules have helped me keep myself fit thus far. The following are some of my secrets for looking younger than my age, as a lot of people tell me!

Diet

A heavy wholesome breakfast is a must. Do not compromise on this meal. Try finding warm and fresh alternatives on the menu for breakfast. Skip the cereal and pasta, no matter how tempting and quick it may sound. Instead, go for healthier options like eggs and whole wheat bread. Have whole fresh fruits and salads instead of having juices or aerated drinks. I know it is a little difficult to keep an eye on the menu when you're in a hurry, but it will go a long way in keeping you healthy.

Do not miss meals. Ensure that you have regular meals at a stipulated time if possible. Avoid the temptation of filling up with fast food during your meals on a frequent basis. Go easy on the caffeine. Keep your intake to maximum of two cups a day, preferably one. You could opt for green tea instead which is a healthier option. Keep a tab on having too much sugary and fried food. Try to eat something every two hours. It need not be a huge meal. Just a handful of nuts should do. Resist the urge to binge on junk food—keep the chips and chocolates out of the way. Treat yourself occasionally with food that you crave, an ice-cream maybe. These tips will not only keep your metabolism in check, but also keep those pesky pimples at bay.

Sleep

No matter what kind of sleep schedule your friends and roommates have, do your best to stick to your own schedule on regular days. A random day of going out and staying up late is okay once in awhile, like on the occasional weekend. But on regular weekdays aim to sleep at the same time every night, latest by 11 p.m. A quick shower before you hit the bed will ensure that the day's weariness is washed away and you will sleep better.

Your advantage of being an early riser is always going to give you an edge above others. Use the tranquility of early mornings to take a stroll or simply relax outdoors if the weather is pleasant. If not outdoors, a balcony or window sill is a good place to chill with your morning cup of coffee.

I usually prefer gazing at the greenery, the skies, or birds. Just sharing a small trivia with you: it is said that gazing at a green color is supposed to be healthy for your eyes and also your mind as it is supposed to have a soothing effect. Those first few thoughts that we reflect on after waking up in the morning are crucial in building a positive mind frame for the day ahead. The same holds true before falling asleep.

Grooming

Every once in awhile, indulge yourself with the luxury of a professional pedicure or massage. Don't forget that a generous slick of sunscreen is a must before you step out. And yes, a spray of deo too. These grooming mantras are no longer limited to women. Men need to take care of themselves too.

Stick to the routine hygiene standards that you have been raised with. When you start living with other people, it is natural to get influenced by their habits.

A sloppy appearance may make you seem less approachable. A neat appearance and smart dressing will never lose its class. A daily bath in the morning is what works for us Indians, and it always will. Offering a quiet prayer after a bath gives peace of mind. Continue doing so, especially since you've been doing it since your childhood.

Always remember, moderation is the key to having a balanced life. Know your limits in everything you do and work accordingly. We live only once, so it doesn't make sense to deprive ourselves of things that we wish to do. However, not going overboard works well in the long run.

No matter how much material wealth we make in life, if we are unable to maintain our health and wellness, we will never be able to enjoy the fruits of our labor. Do everything that your heart longs for, but be mindful of how much and how often you do it. Have a wholesome life my child. May God always keep you strong, healthy, and happy.

Love,
Ma

Working around Xenophobia

Dear Viv,

We've probably not discussed this in depth. That's the reason I felt it was vital for me to bring up this topic in this series of letters. Today I wish to discuss something that you could encounter at some point in your journey ahead. Xenophobia is a dislike of or prejudice against people from other countries. While it does not necessarily mean the same thing as racism, it does have a tinge of racism to it, somehow.

Xenophobia refers to dislike or fear of what is foreign, including people from foreign countries. Racism, on the other hand, is the belief that members of a particular race are better than another due to specific traits. Across the world, there are racial discriminations among people belonging to different groups. They are discriminated against based on their cultural or ethnic beliefs.

Since you might be living amongst people who belong to various cultural backgrounds, you might come across individuals or groups who are xenophobes. I suggest that you do not get dragged into such controversial matters, unless you become a victim of discrimination.

A person of color may have some challenges on this front as they seem to become soft targets in such matters. Only if you experience some direct harm or threat, should you be firm in assertively yet gently confronting the perpetrator.

This should ideally be done when you're with a group of mixed people of different ethnicities who can have a neutral stand on the issue to support you. However since this is a sensitive topic, you need to be extra cautious while talking to the person concerned, with the words you choose and the implication of those words.Explain to them that their behavior towards you is upsetting you. Also make them understand that although you come from a different background, nationality, and culture does not mean that you're any different from them in the way you think.

At all costs avoid a flare-up. Do not get provoked by aggressiveness by them if it comes to that point. And at all costs, avoid being alone during or after the verbal exchange. Beyond that, make a conscious attempt to ignore their behavior if it continues. Understand that these are deep-rooted prejudices that have been ingrained in them by society. It has nothing to do with you personally.

Be proud of who you are no matter what the person has made you feel about yourself. Be the bigger person by letting it go. Be thankful for the fact that you have been raised to be accepting of others, no matter where they come from or what their beliefs are.

I was once involved in a tricky conversation with two work colleagues who belong to different nationalities. The conversation veered towards the hygiene standards of people in this country. One of them asked me why most people in India did not use deodorants since they sweat so much. The other one went on about why we Indians slapped our hair with such strongly smelling oils that stank in the elevators.

While it was all said in in jest, I smiled at them and gently reminded them that it was they who had chosen to come to this country for better prospects. They always had the choice of going back to their own fragrant countries if the stink was getting too much for them to handle. That shut them up, but not before they laughed it off. So sometimes humor and tact can be blended effectively to achieve desired results. Thankfully I never heard from them again on the topic.

Now imagine the same conversation if I was a foreigner in their country. What would I do? I'd probably gift them each a bottle of hair oil. I'd tell them about the benefits of applying it—how it helps people sprout new hair when no other expensive treatments help combat loss of hair issues. And if that doesn't break the ice, I'd simply shut up and pretend to get busy with something else.

You need to weigh the pros and cons of such conversations before indulging in them. If you're unsure about how your words would be received, leave it at that and cut the conversation short. If you sense xenophobic behavior in public places with strangers, do not give it any importance. Avoid eye contact or initiating conversations with the person if you sense their hostility. It would be best to move away from them as fast as possible to avoid any potential outburst.

I sincerely hope that you do not have to ever face any of this. I wonder why people compartmentalize others. It is rather unfortunate that we live in a world that is divided by race, color, and creed. Aim to bridge the gap in interactions with people from other cultures. Understand the virtues of their culture and beliefs. This will help you understand various perspectives and accept others for who they are. It will also broaden your belief system and help you grow as an empathetic individual. That, according to me, will be the highest level of education that you will ever receive.

Love,
Ma

Yearnings of Youth

Dear Viv,

Well you've finally entered the rollercoaster ride of youth from your bratty boyhood. Just what you were waiting for—to grow up and be classified as an adult. I still cannot come to terms with the fact that you're no longer a child. Those naughty prank-filled years of mischief and laughter passed by in a jiffy. I never imagined it to be so short-lived.

As you enter this precious phase, I am reminded of my own glorious years of youth. This age that you're at brings a lot of hopes and yearnings. It might seem as though a new world has opened up to you and in a way, it has. You may want to explore all that your life has restricted you to this point. You may want to experience everything and decide for yourself whether it is good for you or not. Suddenly a lot of taboos seem to have vanished.

It's so exciting to discover that you've grown into a smart young man. You have a circle of friends who are fun to hang out with. There is so much to do with them. You're plagued by a new disease called FOMO, short for 'Fear of Missing Out' on what's new, trendy, and cool. These are some of the things to keep yourself updated with lest you miss out on what makes you acceptable and noticed in your peer group.

You're now sorted out on what you want to do with your future. Well, almost. There are so many things that still confuse you when it comes to settling down on your choice of vocation. You tell yourself that there's still time. You could figure it out along the way. And then suddenly out of nowhere you notice a new interest that catches your attention—girls!

Even though they were always around you never really saw them in this light. Somehow they seem so attractive now. You might find yourself in the company of women who want a chunk of your time and attention or likewise you might start feeling drawn to someone.

There's a hint of subtle and healthy flirting. You're surprised that it actually happened. The feminine qualities you had scorned earlier as vain and frivolous are now what you dig in her. You find it weird, yet interesting. You smile to yourself half the time when you think of it. *"Hell, was I blind all these years that I did not notice how gorgeous they really are?!"*

Time to go out on a date? You want to spruce up your looks and wardrobe, sport a beard, maybe. And spray some manly cologne too. It may be time to apply for a driving license and get a car. After all, you have arrived and you'd rather do it in style!

I keep bringing up the topic of dating for the simple reason that I'm happy that you are your own person. You've noticed lately that a lot of your friends have started dating. I am glad that you don't feel the need to do that just to keep up with your friends. Not that there's anything wrong with it. It can be a wonderful way of getting to know more about the opposite sex, but it needs to happen organically. You don't need to date just because all your friends are. This is the kind of attitude I'd like you to have.

You will cherish the memories of your youth. Never again will you feel as free as you do now with future work and family responsibilities. In the heady excitement of freedom, you may crave to do so many things at one time that sometimes you may tend to go off track. If you analyze carefully, certain choices that you make are an unconscious reflection of what your friends choose or expect you to choose. However this is harmless if you're in good company.

On the other hand, there is a strong possibility that if you happen to mingle with someone who has unhealthy habits or wrong ideologies, it would be detrimental to blindly follow their choices and adapt them. Once you are aware of how different their values are from yours, step back every time you decide to do something that is on the same lines as what that person does. Evaluate carefully if their habit is good for you. Even if you feel that there is no harm in going ahead with it, simply ask yourself if you could do without it.

For example, at some point you might have to share a room with someone who smokes. While you always kept your head above water, when you're in close proximity with people who have such habits, you might be tempted to give it a try sometime. You might have resisted giving into it, but someday your curiosity might take over and urge you to try it just once. A single drag maybe. And you feel that the act of billowing smoke rings out of your mouth makes you look a tad cool. Be warned though that it is these first-time trials that can lead to a lifetime of wrong habits that one is not able to give up easily. The supposedly cool and happening habit turns into a life-threatening addiction in a matter of time.

The same goes for spending habits. You may notice some of your friends who are extravagant. They're wearing the priciest brands, driving the swankiest cars, and splurging on regular clubbing. That probably is the lifestyle that they have been brought up with or have found an affinity to. Your Dad and I did our best to give you all that you ever wished for in your childhood, everything that was within our means and good for you.

The same guidelines should also apply now. No matter what lifestyle those you associate with have, it is not necessary to blindly follow them. Mob mentality is often the trait of people who do not evaluate their thoughts and actions. A few indulgences here and there are understandable, but make sure that you're not unconsciously doing things in order to fit in. You are free to make changes once you are financially independent and mature enough to know what works for you. Until that time, know your boundaries.

Stand true to who you are. Go with the flow but make conscious choices. You'll realize that there is a right time for everything. Analyze each desire before you decide to surrender to it. This is the time to enjoy your youth in the best possible way, but with a surety that it does not haunt you in your later years. I do hope you enjoy your prime days to the hilt and make them last forever. After all, you're never too old to be young!

Love,
Ma

The Zeal to Live Life to the Fullest

Dear Viv,

This is my last letter to you in this series. Wow! It feels as though I have been yapping since eternity! Jokes aside, I hope my letters have resonated with you. You said you liked the philosophical tone in my words when you read the very first letter. That was such a huge relief! I dreaded that you'd find these topics serious and boring.

The last thing I am writing to you about is the zeal to live life. The dictionary describes the meaning of the word zeal as "*great energy or enthusiasm in pursuit of a cause or an objective*."

I've already touched upon the importance of charting out future goals and objectives, but that's not enough. To achieve targets, one needs to go for them with a great deal of ardor to bring out optimal results. I think to have zest in life has more to do with enriching oneself with new interests, tapping into fresh resources to update oneself, and filling up time with meaningful activities to add value to our lives. Only this has to be pursued to feed our soul, and nourished with renewed energy that these feel-good activities pump into our being. We notice from the glint in someone's eye if they have been up to something new that they've thoroughly enjoyed. That adrenaline rush is the best part about having a passion in life.

A long time ago even before you were born, your Dad used to cook every Sunday. He had never formally learned cooking, but had done quite a few trials and errors in the kitchen to know the basics. He would rustle up a special dish with a lot of verve, making it a point to experiment with the seasonings and flavors. With every bit of patience, he would let the gravy simmer and watch his dish cook in its juices with great pride. And when he would present it onto the table, there would be a look of great anticipation gleaming in his eyes, waiting for the expected word of appreciation. Somewhere along the line as life got busier, his interest died a slow death. And along with his passion in cooking, I saw a gradual decline in his interest levels in general. I'm sure if he revived his love for cooking, you would be able to see the brilliance of enthusiasm that I saw in his eyes years ago.

As long as we remain passionate, which we normally are in our younger days, we continue to live with fervor even as we grow older. However, it is possible that over a period of time our spirits may start to fizzle out. We can consciously work on it by making certain lifestyle changes to charge ourselves back into action.

People have trouble identifying that they have even lost their spark. Today you turn all of 18. My heart swells with pride to see the evolved adult that you have grown up into. Your proactiveness and healthy interest in enriching yourself fill me with great hope for a wonderful future. I only wish with all my heart that I never see your bright spirit ever getting dim in the din of everyday life.

Before you start assuming the responsibilities of a professional, a spouse, and a father in future, remember that besides these new roles that you will don, you have an independent personality which should not dissipate in the whirl of worldly responsibility. No one but you yourself are responsible to keep the fire burning within you. Make time for yourself without feeling guilty about it. Do things that you've never done before if they strike a chord with you. Do not care about what others have to say about it. If something tickles your senses go for it without a second thought. Dare to be different and do not fret if you're not. Sometimes ordinary traits can also yield extraordinary results!

I have observed some of the most successful people evolving by the sheer magic of their zealousness. Some of the most out-of-box thinkers have turned into innovative entrepreneurs, making their success stories unique. They wouldn't have reached where they are without nurturing their dynamism. Such people are always on a lookout for the unexplored. I've jotted down some ideas that I believe could help you maintain your zest for life.

Take risks – You can only discover treasures when you dive deep into the sea. Take the plunge.

Do new things – Developing new interests keeps boredom from setting in.

Surround yourself with a wide variety of inspiring people – I say wide variety because there's so much out there to learn from different kinds of people. Don't limit yourself to only one type.

Do not conform to set standards of society – Be your own person. You are setting your own standards only for yourself and not for social acceptance.

Do not overanalyze every minor detail of your life – Sometimes we spoil the magic of the moment by thinking too much about minor issues. Go with the flow and let the situation pass without much thought.

Travel by yourself – Take off on a solo trip once in awhile. Traveling on your own gives you new insights and wisdom.

Read voraciously – Read different genres. They help you broaden your perspective.

Savor the present moment – Being mindful of the present is the key to truly squeezing out the best out of each moment.

Ever-ready to learn – The lessons never stop if you look for them. It is the seeking that makes you wiser.

Keep yourself flexible – Routine is boring. Being flexible gives you the opportunity to break away from routine.

Don't take life too seriously – Look at the lighter side in all situations. It definitely makes life much more fun.

Every now and then it helps to sit and retrospect. Make a note of what you have achieved so far and what is it that you would like to go for in the days to come. A bucket list comes handy in this case. Make short-term plans on how you're going to make your life more interesting. These plans are like tiny doses of treats to keep your fire burning.

By the end of the last letter, I would like to request you to keep these letters with you as a handy book and refer to them if you ever find yourself stuck in a particular situation. I sincerely hope that you're able to find most of your answers in them.

I've done my bit by getting you into this world and trying to raise you with the right values infused with the right amount of zest. Now the responsibility of carrying the values forward in a healthy manner lies with you. Rise and grow, first of all in your eyes and the rest will fall into place. Keep the hunger for zeal in your life alive and kicking as that's the way I wish to see my seeker-son digging out the treasures of life.

Infinite love and tight warm hugs. God bless you my child.

Love,
Ma

Epilogue

My son turned 20 recently. It's been a couple of years since I wrote this series of letters to him. He tells me that he turns to these letters, even today, when he's confused about something, looking for advice or simply when he misses me. I felt I should write one more letter, on his birthday to look back since he ventured out on his own.

Dear Viv,

Wishing you a Happy 20th Birthday!

Welcome to the 20s! Congratulations on sailing through the tumultuous teens smoothly and patiently. I must add that you will miss the excitement of these growing years, and so will I.

These past two years simply zoomed by. From the time I accompanied a young unsure teen to his new environs in a new country, to the responsible, self-assured, and adaptable young man that I see today—stop gloating!—this journey of yours only seems to be getting highly interesting with time.

Ever since you landed overseas, we have had our share of hair pulling in frustration, figuring out a lot of things along the way, some anticipated and some not. I think this made us grow even more. I say that because we both learned and grew in the process.

It is also me learning to let go and trusting you to handle things on your own. They say that the umbilical cord never really gets severed. An invisible cord always connects the mother with her child despite the distance that separates them. The biggest challenge a mother faces is to loosen the grip on this cord to facilitate her child to become independent. In the past few months I feel that I have been able to do that, sometimes consciously and sometimes because there was no other choice.

It wasn't easy of course in the beginning. For example, I fretted about what you ate, and why you suddenly decided to go off dairy. I also wondered, how would you remain strong and healthy without getting your daily dose of calcium? I anxiously hoped that you would get the last bus back to campus after a night out with friends. I scolded you when you forgot to send me the confirmatory ping in the middle of the night to let me know that you were back safely in your dorm. I also fretted about the friends you made. I wished that you had made more Indian friends to at least satiate your taste buds with Indian food that you so crave. I chewed my nails praying that you did not fall ill and covered yourself with thick warm clothes when it started to snow. I wondered if you chose the right subjects. I also hoped that you continued to research new courses to be in line with your future goals. I lost sleep on nights waiting to know the results of your tests and exams. I also was concerned if you had packed your luggage properly and made it in time to take the flight back home. You chided me to go back to sleep at three in the morning, while I battled the time zone difference with bleary eyes just to make sure that things were all right with you.

Sometimes you must have felt that I came on quite strongly trying to push you into doing stuff. That was actually my way of ensuring that you did not make mistakes or leave loose ends. There were things that you were doing differently, some of which I didn't wholly approve of. You once told me when I tried to correct you that you wanted to make your own mistakes. So well, I decided to go ahead and let you make them, and for once figure it out for yourself. I am glad you're ready to take the onus for your mistakes and are honest enough to correct them when required.

Thankfully most of my anxieties were laid to rest, when I saw the way you slowly adjusted yourself to get in tune with your new routine. I noticed all the effort you put into doing so and I secretly admired you for it. After all this was new to you, being a single child who had never been left on his own.

It was reassuring to know that you shopped for groceries, cooked, and ate your share of greens as well as studied hard, hung out with bright friends, and scored exceptionally great. And all this while taking care of yourself. I am sure you know who's the proudest mum in the world! I can't even begin to describe how a parent feels when they see their child starting to look after themselves.

I still do worry and obsess about the tiniest challenges that come your way, but from what I've observed over the last few months, you somehow manage them, sometimes a tad clumsily and other times beautifully. It also gives me great comfort to know that you have been referring to my letters periodically and that they gave you solace during trying times. At least these letters are there with you, wording my thoughts at every step you take. In time you might not require my gentle admonishing or guidance to get through obstacles, but well, I doubt if I will ever stop looking over you! That's what mothers are for, right?

This is the perfect day for me to tell you how grateful I am with the way you are evolving.

I love you so much. May God continue to bless you with an abundance of happiness, good health, and success. Make a wish as you blow out your birthday candles, count your blessings, and have lots of fun. You absolutely deserve it for all the hard work and resilience that you have displayed.

Happy Birthday Sweetheart!

Big hugs and lots of love,
Ma

Acknowledgements

My son Viven, the soul of this book and the love of my life—you made this happen. Thanks for brainstorming every small detail of this book with me and making this about us.

To my parents who are my strength and the foundation of my writing journey. Thanks to my mother for encouraging me to push my boundaries and my father for always believing in me. I'm grateful to Venkat for bringing Viven into my life. Love to my brother, Satish, for reaching across the seven seas to extend his unwavering support in all my endeavors as always. To Sreeram and Upendra who complete my family. I would like to thank Viven's cousins and friends who have been a part of his growing up.

Thanks to Elly Stornebrink, a dear friend of mine whom I initially met through an online blogging community. When I asked her to "look over" my manuscript, she agreed to use her professional expertise to do so, initially without my knowledge. I am deeply indebted to her for her valuable time and invaluable editing expertise.

I'd like to give a special mention to one of the most creative teenagers I have ever come across. Aruvi Dave, a student of architecture, has brought the book cover to life with her colorful imagination. She has a brilliant flair for art and design. To get the book cover designed by such a talented teen, for a book dedicated to teens seems apt to me. I would also like to thank Zaida Jacob, Aruvi's mother, and my close friend, for providing her unique perspective and inputs for the book cover design as well as the content.

Thanks to Nirav Sanghvi for providing his invaluable suggestions. To Mruduk Pathak Kundu for sharing her views. I am thankful to Preethi Venugopala for her support.

My sincere gratitude to my readers and friends from the blogging world for their honest feedback and recommendations that helped me shape these letters into a book.

Thanks to Bibhu Rout, Divya Mirchandani, Hitesh Jain, Prashant Gurav, Yogesh Desai and the entire team of StoryMirror Publications. They have been exceptionally supportive and patient with me.

To the friends, colleagues, and acquaintances I may have referred to in the letters (with identities and situations tweaked, of course). Each of you have contributed to my journey in your own small way.

My heartfelt thanks for the appreciation and morale boosting that comes from my family, friends, and loved ones—you know who you are. This book would not have been possible without the support and encouragement of each and every one of you.

About the Author

Vinodini Parimi is a mother to a nerdy 20-year old computer science student cum aspiring cinematographer from Baroda. She is a design professional who reconnected with her childhood love for writing.

This is her solo debut as an author. Her short stories, "Luscious Aspirations" for *Blank Space* and "Beyond Eternity" for *A Little Chorus of Love* were published in anthologies in 2015. Her travelogues were featured in *Musafir*, a coffee table book published by Nirvana Foundation, Mumbai, in 2018. She writes on parenting, self-help, fashion, travel, and fiction on her website ifsbutsandsetcs.com. She also freelances as a content writer for various brands, portals, and websites.

When she's not busy obsessing over her son's six-pack abs in-the-making, she loves to decode people, doodle on paper napkins after eating without counting calories.

Instagram: https://www.instagram.com/vinodiniparimi

Twitter: https://twitter.com/vinodini

Facebook: https://www.facebook.com/vinodiniparimiauthorpage

www.ingramcontent.com/pod-product-compliance
Lightning Source LLC
Chambersburg PA
CBHW050019170726
48282CB00025B/466
* 9 7 8 9 3 8 8 6 9 8 1 2 2 *